The Measurement of Writing Ability

by Fred I. Godshalk

Frances Swineford

William E. Coffman

Educational Testing Service

College Entrance Examination Board, New York, 1966

Research Monograph Series

Titles available as of January 1973:

(6) The Measurement of Writing Ability. Fred I. Godshalk,
Frances Swineford, and William E. Coffman.
92 pages (1966) $2.50

(5) Personality Measures in Admissions: Antecedent and
Personality Factors as Predictors of College Success.
Morris I. Stein. 76 pages (1963) $2.50

(4) Career Development: Self-Concept Theory.
Donald E. Super, Reuben Starishevsky,
Norman Matlin, and Jean Pierre Jordaan.
100 pages (1963) $2.50

(3) Career Development: Choice and Adjustment.
David V. Tiedeman and Robert P. O'Hara.
115 pages (1963) $2.50

(2) Organizational Measurement and its Bearing
on the Study of College Environments.
Allen H. Barton; Introduction by P. F. Lazarsfeld.
91 pages (1961) $2.50

(1) The Validation of a Biographical Inventory as a
Predictor of College Success. Anne Anastasi,
Martin J. Meade, and Alexander A. Schneiders.
86 pages (1960) $2.50

Inquiries regarding this publication should be addressed to
Editorial Office, College Entrance Examination Board, 888
Seventh Avenue, New York, New York 10019.

Copies of this publication may be ordered from College
Board Publication Orders, Box 2815, Princeton, New
Jersey 08540. The price is $2.50 per copy.

Cover photograph by Glenn Foss

Contents

Introduction iv
Acknowledgments vii
List of tables viii

1. The problem 1

2. Plan and procedure 6
   Testing materials 6
   Criterion materials 8
   The testing population and the sample . . 9
   Procedure 9

3. The criterion 12

4. Relations between predictors and the
   criterion 17
   Data based on total sample 17
   Validities involving a verbal score 19
   Validities in relation to level of ability . . 21
   Validity of an English Composition Test
   that includes an essay 26

5. The field trial 29

6. The measurement of writing ability—
   a significant breakthrough? 39

Bibliography 43
Appendix A. Participating schools, supervisors,
   and teachers 45
Appendix B. Appendix tables 47

Introduction

The measurement of a student's ability to write has been a perplexing problem to the College Board ever since 1901, when its first examinations were offered. The importance of this monograph, *The Measurement of Writing Ability*, lies in the fact that it presents evidence that this problem has at long last been solved, insofar as the current English Composition Tests are concerned. This monograph is the successful culmination of a long series of efforts to evaluate the validity of the College Board's English Composition Test. Great credit must go to the authors—Godshalk, Swineford, and Coffman—both for the ingenuity of their research plans and for the clarity with which their results are set forth.

Measurement of composition as such began to be a special problem for College Board readers when the Comprehensive Examination in English (in use from 1916 to 1940) included an hour's essay along with two hours of questions on books the candidates had read and on unfamiliar passages of prose and poetry printed in the examination itself. Though the reliability of reading the entire paper reached a very respectable level (.88 in 1939), this came about partly because it was possible to reread the essay section when its score was incongruous with the more accurate grades on the other two parts of the paper.

When World War II put an end to the old three-hour Comprehensive Examinations, and a new series of one-hour Achievement Tests replaced them, the test in English became one of composition only. At first, the examiners tried to carry over their experience with the third part of the Comprehensive Examination: the test was simply an hour's essay on a required subject. It was read analytically: that is, a specified range of grades was allotted to each of various components of writing ability—spelling, diction, organization, and so on—and the final raw score on the essay was the sum of these separate grades. In spite of the careful way in which the reading was designed, the grades assigned by a single reader proved unreliable. The separate judgments on from seven to nine components did not improve the reliability of the total score. Relatively few books could be reread, because of the pressure for rapid transmission of grades to colleges. Hence, the candidate's grade in English composition tended to depend far too much on which reader happened to have scored his essay.

Fairness to all candidates has always been a goal of the College Board. A series of experiments—a one-hour essay, three 20-minute essays, four 15-minute paragraphs, read analytically—all proved disappointing. Gradually and reluctantly the examiners (all English teachers and predisposed to essay questions) turned to objective items. These, at least, could be scored with complete accuracy; in time, the English Composition Test became—as it still is in some of its forms—wholly objective.

Before long, the outcry began. By what right could a test which involved no writing whatever be called a test of composition? Further, what would happen to the teaching of writing in the schools, when teachers and students alike knew that writing had vanished from the College Board's Admissions Testing Program? In answer to this outcry, the Board tried another experiment—the General Composition Test—a two-hour essay, with carefully structured topics, and again, given careful, analytical reading. Alas, it proved no better than the earlier one-hour essays; colleges were reluctant to require it; therefore it was dropped from the program.

The abandonment of the General Composition Test, however, increased the pressures for reintroduction of some writing into the testing program. For a while, the committees, trustees, and staff of the Board withstood this pressure, conscious as they were of past failures to read essays with satisfactory reliability. Eventually, a compromise was voted into the program by the membership. This was the Writing Sample: an hour's essay on a topic selected by a committee of examiners, written under test conditions at regular administrations, but not graded by Board readers. Instead, copies were forwarded to the candidates' schools and to designated colleges. Like most compromises, this scheme was not wholly satisfactory to many people. Schools and candidates were unhappy because in many instances they did not know what happened to the Writing Samples at the colleges, or what part they played in the final admissions decisions. They did know that there was wide variation in the way the colleges treated the essays.

Meanwhile, the examiners in English composition had devised a semi-objective section called the interlinear exercise, in which students were asked to discover and amend, by writing between the lines, errors deliberately introduced into a passage of prose. Two criticisms of this item were made: one, that it was bad pedagogy to expose students to writing which contained more, and more flagrant, errors than they themselves were likely to perpetrate; and two, that the exercise was merely a job of editing, proving nothing about the student's ability to write when left to himself.

The examiners believed that the interlinear and the objective sections of the test were more effective than their critics asserted, but they lacked proof. They asked the College Board to authorize studies which would show how valid the various items actually were in their measurement of writing ability. The monograph which follows is one result of that request. The research carried out by experts at Educational Testing Service fully justifies the instinctive confidence the examiners had felt in the tests they were building.

The monograph itself is so clear that any detailed summary here is supererogatory. It is enough to say that, checked against a criterion far more reliable than the usual criteria of teachers' ratings or school and college grades, all but one of the item types currently used in the English Composition Test proved to be excellent predictors; that a very high correlation was achieved when, for a typical one-hour test, two objective item types were combined with an interlinear exercise; and that a 20-minute essay—read, not analytically, but impressionistically and independently by three readers—contributed somewhat more than even the interlinear exercise to the validity of the total score. The combination of objective items (which measure accurately some skills involved in writing) with an essay (which measures directly, if somewhat less accurately, the writing itself) proved to be more valid than either type of item alone. This discovery may well have important implications for testing in subjects other than English composition.

It is clear from this monograph that colleges can in general accept scores on the English Composition Test in any of its current forms as valid indices of their candidates' ability to write. No test is infallible; there will always be some exceptions. Perhaps one word of warning needs to be said: colleges should not expect any higher correlation between English Composition Test scores and college grades in English than there ever has been. For college grades in English cover much more than the student's ability to write: they may include his comprehension of and sensitivity to literature, his attentiveness in class, his penmanship or typing, and his ability to get assignments in on time. Then, too, grades are likely to vary from one instructor to another. This test, however, focuses solely on the student's ability to write. Its success is proved by its high correlation with a criterion of writing ability uncontaminated by any of the other considerations which go into college grades. How that criterion was created and used is not the least important and interesting portion of the monograph.

Edward S. Noyes
Special consultant to the president
College Entrance Examination Board

Acknowledgments

An investigation of this magnitude requires the labor of many individuals other than the principal investigators. We cannot hope to remember and acknowledge our debt to everyone who has made a contribution. We are, however, keenly conscious of our debt to the many people who shared their insights with us by publishing the results of their research. We consider this monograph one in a continuing series of studies which is expanding our understanding of the problems of the measurement of writing skills.

We owe special thanks also to Edward S. Noyes, who offered encouragement during the planning stage and who prepared a preliminary report for publication in the *College Board Review;* to Henry S. Dyer, who gave his approval to the project in spite of skepticism regarding the validity of our idea for developing a criterion measure and who prodded us to complete this report when it would have been easy to plead the pressure of other work; to the various members of the College Board's Committee of Examiners in English, who over the years have contributed to the development of the many ideas embodied in the several predictors used in the study; to the readers, who brought their professional skills to the task of judging the qualities of the essays; and to Marian Tyson and Joan M. Holeman of Educational Testing Service, who attended to the many clerical details of preparing the manuscript.

Finally, we acknowledge the contributions of the many people at Educational Testing Service and the College Entrance Examination Board with whom we discussed the project and the contributions of teachers and students without whose efforts no data could have been collected.

Fred I. Godshalk
Frances Swineford
William E. Coffman

Tables

Page

1. Analysis of variance of the essay reading and estimates of reading reliability and of test reliability of total essay score 12
2. Means and standard deviations of scores on the five readings of each of five essay topics 14
3. Average correlations between single readings within essay topics and across essay topics 15
4. Correlations between total scores on the five readings of each essay topic (estimates of reading reliabilities are shown in parentheses). 15
5. Correlations of English Composition Test subtest scores with the sum of five scores on each essay and with the total essay score 17
6. Validity of selected combinations of subtest scores. 18
7. Subgroup means and standard deviations . 19
8. Validity estimates of selected sums (X) of subtest scores and of best weighted combinations of X and PSAT-verbal or SAT-verbal scores 20
9. Means and standard deviations for senior and junior groups scoring high and low on "usage" 22
10. Correlations of English Composition Test subtest scores and PSAT-verbal scores with total essay score for junior and senior groups scoring low and high on "usage" . . 23
11. Validity estimates of sums (X) of subtest scores and of best weighted combinations of X and PSAT-verbal scores for high and low groups 25
12. Multiple correlations for selected sets of predictors 27
13. Design for reading English essays—December 1962 31
14. Estimates of reading reliabilities of essay ratings 32
15. Estimates of score reliabilities of essay ratings 33
16. Summary of correlations of objective English scores, field-trial essay scores, and PSAT-verbal scores with four-essay, 20-reading criterion of writing ability 34
17. Correlations of field-trial scores (four readings) and original scores (five readings) on topics A and B with independent four-topic, 20-reading criterion of writing ability . . 35
18. Reading reliabilities, score reliabilities, and test validities of sums of four field-trial readings 35
19. Multiple correlations of selected combinations of predictors with four-essay, 20-reading criterion of writing ability . . . 37

The problem

The studies reported in this monograph began as an investigation of the relative validity of different approaches to the measurement of English composition skills. These approaches were developed at Educational Testing Service between 1945 and 1960 in response to an increasing pressure for efficient and reliable procedures which might be applied to large-scale testing programs. Various questions were raised which led to special analyses of the data collected and to the collection of additional data. Of particular interest was Miss Swineford's recognition that the data might be analyzed in such a way as to provide evidence regarding the validity of a 20-minute essay as well as of other types of questions. What began as a study of limited scope and sharp focus expanded into a comprehensive investigation of the measurement of composition skills.

The first analyses were designed to assess the relative validities of the interlinear exercise and of several types of multiple-choice questions. The interlinear exercise is a structured, free-response exercise which can be read with high reliability by trained readers; however, it is costly to process. Answers to two questions were sought: How did validity coefficients for the interlinear exercise compare with those for other kinds of questions? In combination with other questions in a one-hour English Composition Test, did the interlinear exercise make a unique contribution or was it possible to achieve equivalent results by the use of combinations of objective questions only?

As the studies proceeded, two additional questions became of concern: Did the relative validity of a type of question vary with the level of ability of the candidate group? Did a 20-minute essay compare favorably with other types of questions or was it so unreliable that it could not compete?

The criterion against which various types of questions were validated consisted of five work samples of free writing. These samples were to be produced under controlled conditions. They would be so devised and graded as to define writing competency in terms of the product created by writers with a wide range of skill, and the results judged by a panel of qualified critics. The procedure was intended to produce a reliable criterion by the summation of several independent judgments of each paper, combined to produce a great many judgments of the total performance of each writer.

It will be seen that the criterion devised for this study is one which provides not only a measure of writing ability but an operational definition of writing ability, as well. In this respect, at least, the experiment was to become something more than just another of the many validity studies conducted in the past. Previous studies had used grades, or ratings, or single essays as criteria. A major problem, however, existed in the attempt to create the criterion, for the procedure itself was experimental. To avoid problems of reading reliability and the burden of a slow analytical reading, it was proposed that readings be holistic—that is, that readers be asked to make a single judgment with little or no guidance as to detailed standards. General standards of a "too high" or "too low" sort would be established by having a group of readers rate selected papers independently and then compare scores. In this manner it was assumed that readers would adjust their individual expectations of quality to the standards of the group of readers.

As has been implied, we did not come to this study completely lacking in knowledge regarding the validity of the various types of questions in the different forms of the English Composition Test. Problems of reliability and validity had been faced by the Committees of Examiners, at least since Hopkins (1921) demonstrated that the score a student made on a College Board examination might well depend more on which year he appeared for the examination, or on which person read his paper, than it would on what he had written.

The problems became particularly severe following the introduction of one-hour tests of achievement in the early 1940s. In 1945, Noyes, Sale, and Stalnaker (1947) reviewed the data from six different one-hour essay examinations and concluded that the reliability of the reading had been too low to meet College Board standards. For two of the tests the reading reliability had been .58 and .59 and in only one case had the reading reliability exceeded .69. Experiments during subsequent years with three or four short essays instead of one long essay were equally frustrating.

Meanwhile, progress was being made in the development of objective and semi-objective measures which might be expected to measure some of the component skills of writing ability. Huddleston (1954) compared the validities of the verbal section of the Scholastic Aptitude Test (SAT) and of an objective editing test with those for essay ratings based on two paragraphs composed by the students. The criteria were English grades and systematic ratings of writing ability made by teachers who knew the students well. The correlations between SAT-verbal scores and the criteria were so high (.76 with ratings and .77 with grades) that there was little room for improvement by adding other measures. The objective editing exercise did raise the correlations .03, however, and Huddleston concluded that a combination of SAT-verbal scores and objective English scores provided the best prediction available at that time.

Diederich (1950) investigated the relative effectiveness of these same types of questions and other types using samples from Phillips Exeter Academy and the Choate School. The criterion was ratings of writing ability by teachers using an 18-point scale ranging from A+ to F−. In general, Diederich's findings were similar to Huddleston's except that the English Composition Test contributed somewhat more and the verbal sections of the SAT somewhat less to the multiple correlations. The SAT-verbal score was still the best single predictor. For the Choate School sample, the second best predictor was a 40-minute essay which had been rated on a 10-point scale by one of four experienced readers. Little significance was attached to this finding, for Diederich commented, "It was not judged worthwhile to ascer-

in the precise [reliability] figures because the reliability attained by these four readers could never be duplicated by the 60 or 70 readers who must be used in scoring a national examination."

Spurred by the evidence of validity for objective and semi-objective questions, a number of people devoted effort to the refinement of techniques during the period from 1950 to 1960. Swineford and Olsen (1953) reported satisfactory reliability and validity for the interlinear exercise, which will be described later. Coffman and Papachristou (1955) reported preliminary success with a number of types of questions designed on the basis of an analysis of student essays. Thomas (1956) succeeded in adapting Stalaker's construction shift question to a machine-scorable format. Miller (1953) pointed out the great variety of skills tested by the interlinear exercise. Weiss (1957) demonstrated that several of the types of questions used in the College Board English Composition Test were making distinctive contributions to the prediction of college English grades. The types of questions chosen for use in this study, therefore, had been developed through intense scholarly effort and were superior to those available at the time Huddleston and Diederich had made their investigations about 12 to 14 years before.

In spite of the growing evidence that the objective and semi-objective English composition questions were valid, teachers and administrators in schools and colleges kept insisting that candidates for admission to college ought to be required to demonstrate their writing skill directly. In 1953 experimentation was begun on a two-hour General Composition Test, but Pearson (1955) reported that it had proved no more reliable than the shorter essay examinations used in earlier years. By 1960 a Writing Sample, copies of which were transmitted directly to the colleges without central grading, was competing with the English Composition Test for candidates' time.

It had become apparent that the group of candidates taking the English Composition Test would continue to expand so that instead of the 60 to 70 readers mentioned by Diederich in 1950, one could anticipate the use of 300 or 400 readers simply to grade an interlinear exercise. Because there was little evidence that critics of the test were willing to accept the interlinear exercise as a substitute for free writing, was it really worth the cost? Weiss had shown that it did make a distinctive contribution to prediction of English grades, but the contribution was so small as to be of little practical significance.

On the other hand, the small size of the contribution might result primarily from the fact that freshman English grades are not satisfactory criteria of writing ability. Of course, to the extent that writing skill is either assumed at the outset of the course, or taught further in various freshman courses, certain degrees of skill become prerequisites to successful performance in the course. But it must be obvious that a test of composition skill cannot be equally valid in all colleges as a predictor of performance in freshman English. Very few, if any, courses in required freshman English, are devoted to composition exclusively; furthermore, the emphasis upon composition skill differs a great deal from one institution to another and even from class to class within a single institution. Hence the attempt to validate the English Composition Test on the basis of the success of students in the freshman English courses of various colleges creates a situation that is logically unsound. Grades in English rest on a composite behavior of which writing skill is only one part, and often a small part.

What is needed, then, for a validity study of the English Composition Test is a logically sound criterion of composition skill. Such a criterion would be shorn of many extraneous and confusing outcomes of instruction in English courses, including reading skill, speaking skill, the appreciation of literature, and even the habit of getting assigned work done on time. Again it must be obvious that none of these aspects of typical English courses is germane to the testing problem—a problem that may be stated as follows: How well does each student write? How valid is the English Composition Test as a measure of each student's ability to write?

At the time the study was designed, it was known that the unreliability of essay tests came from two major sources: the differences in quality of student writing from one topic to another, and the differences among readers in what they consider the characteristics of good writing. The first source of error could be reduced by having students write on a number of different topics. Thus, an individual's rating would not depend on whether or not he could find something interesting and accurate to say on a single topic

which he might never have considered before. The second source of error could be reduced by having the papers read by a number of different readers.

During the 1940s, when serious efforts were being made to improve the reliability of reading of essays, attempts were made to train readers in making a detailed analysis of each essay. Coward (1950) had thrown serious doubts on the superiority of analytical reading over holistic reading. Experience with the General Composition Test confirmed these doubts. It looked as if the efforts to improve reading reliability had been going in the wrong direction. The solution, it seemed, was in subjecting each paper to the judgment of a number of different readers. The consensus would constitute a valid measure of writing ability, assuming, of course, that the readers were competent.

There was some evidence to support this belief. A study by Diederich, French, and Carlton (1961) had demonstrated that readers of essays fell into five clusters depending on whether they gave primary weight to "mechanics," "ideas," "reasoning," "form," or "flavor" in grading essays. At the same time, the five clusters were far from independent. Readers who favored one characteristic of writing were also giving some weight to other aspects of writing. In other words, the factors were correlated. According to the data, the average intercorrelation among the readings was .31; and these readers had neither met together nor undergone any special training for the job. A little calculation indicated that the sum of 20 of these readings would produce a reading reliability

.90. With a modest period of training readers
ight be able to read more reliably. In fact, Ander-
on (1960) had reported a score reliability, that is, a
orrelation between two different topics of .451 with
ach topic read by a different reader. The sum of such
ores over 11 topics would produce a score reliabil-
y of .90. Anderson's work made use of the Sequen-
al Tests of Educational Progress (STEP) essay tests.
he tests had been constructed at ETS, and the scor-
g method recommended was one which made use
holistic judgments.

On the basis of the data reported by Diederich,
rench, and Carlton, and by Anderson, it was esti-
ated that if five carefully chosen topics were as-
gned and each read by five different readers, a score
liability of at least .80 and a reading reliability of at
ast .90 could be expected. The cost of developing
ch a criterion measure would be high, but con-
dering the importance of the problem, it did not
em unreasonable. We proceeded with the design of
e study.

2. Plan and procedure

The plan of the study called for the administration of eight experimental tests and five essay topics to a sample of secondary school juniors and seniors and for relating scores on the tests to ratings on the essays. The tests, the essay topics, the samples, and the procedures for administering and scoring the tests and essays are described in this chapter. The analyses of the data are described in Chapters 3 and 4.

Testing materials

a. *Objective items.* The six classes of objective items used in the study are identified for purposes of convenience by the terms usage, sentence correction, paragraph organization, prose groups, error recognition, and construction shift. Each of these was represented by a 20-minute section of a test.

(1) Usage items require the recognition of faulty usage, including grammar, diction, basic structure, and mechanics, although the last two points are not often tested in the items now used.

Example:

He spoke <u>bluntly</u> and <u>angrily</u> to <u>we spectators</u>.
(A) bluntly   (B) angrily   (C) we   (D) spectators   (E) No error

(2) Sentence correction items require the selection of a best form for an underlined portion of a sentence. Typically they test sentence structure, although simple grammar, diction, and mechanics may also be included in the testing material.

Example:

<u>While waving</u> goodbye to our friends, the airplane took off, and we watched it disappear in the sky.
(A) While waving   (B) Upon waving   (C) Having waved   (D) Waving   (E) While we waved

(3) The paragraph organization type requires the student to reassemble several "scrambled" sentences into a coherent paragraph and to show the correct order of sentences.

Example:

(A) A sharp distinction must be drawn between table manners and sporting manners.
(B) This kind of handling of a spoon at the table, however, is likely to produce nothing more than an angry protest against squirting grapefruit juice about.
(C) Thus, for example, a fly ball caught by an outfielder in baseball or a completed pass in football is a subject for applause.
(D) Similarly, the dexterous handling of a spoon in golf to release a ball from a sand trap may win a championship match.
(E) But a biscuit or a muffin tossed and caught at the table produces scorn and reproach.

The student is required to answer questions concerning the position of each sentence. The "correct" order in this case is (A), (C), (E), (D), (B).

(4) Prose groups consist of sets of items, each based upon a paragraph with a sentence omitted. For

ch of four sentences that might supply the omis-
on, the student is required to judge whether it is ap-
ropriate, deficient in sense, inadequate in tone or
ction, or deficient because of grammar or construc-
on.

Example:

In the restless chill of the city night, Mr. Brown found it hard to sleep and asked himself, "What is the good of talk? As it is, there are too many opinions in the world. . . . Some want money and others a seat in heaven."

(A) Nobody knows what he wants or where he is going.
(B) Everybody has his own ideas and wants to profit by them.
(C) Everybody thinks they know what they want and how to get rich by it.
(D) Everybody has his own illusions and wants to promulgate them to his own advantage.

(5) Error recognition items require the student to cide whether a sentence is free from error of the nds described, or if not, to indicate which of four asses of error it illustrates: faulty diction, verbosity redundancy, clichés or abused metaphors, or ulty grammar or structure.

Examples:

1. The audience was strongly effected by the senator's speech.
2. In those days there was then no right of petition.
3. Before nightfall the attacking force had gained a foothold in the heart of the defensive fortifications.
4. The commission decided to reimburse the property owners, to readjust the rates, and that they would extend the services in the near future.

(6) The construction shift item requires the student to decide what additional changes to make in a sentence if a specified element is changed in a certain way. The original sentence does not contain an error or problem; the purpose of the item is to test the ability to manipulate elements of the sentence.

Example:

Statements such as "this picture is trash" or "the outlook is dark" or "this steak is wonderful" are statements not only about the picture, the outlook, or the steak but also about the speaker's reaction to them.

Directions: Substitute give less information for are statements not only.

Your rewritten sentence will contain which of the following:

(A) but about   (B) as about   (C) than about
(D) than the   (E) and more about

b. *Interlinear exercises.* The interlinear exercise consists of poorly written material that requires the student to find and correct deficiencies. The two interlinear exercises used were chosen primarily because of the possibility that differences in understanding of kinds of material might affect the corrections made. One exercise was largely narrative and detailed the hardships at Valley Forge during the Revolution. The other exercise was expository with a discussion and explanation of some of the characteristics of the housefly. Both interlinear exercises, like the objective sections, had been used in regular administrations of the tests and possessed known statistical characteristics as well as detailed scoring requirements.

Example:

Never had the fortunes of England ~~dived~~ *fallen* to a lower ebb than at the moment when Elizabeth ~~ascends~~ *ascended* the throne. The country was humiliated by defeat, *torn by* dissension, ~~had torn it~~, and ~~it was being~~ threatened by ~~hosts of~~ danger from without. ~~The~~ ~~England's~~ ~~English~~ hope lay in ~~their~~ *her* queen. ~~Not only~~ ~~was~~ Elizabeth *was* the daughter of Henry but the daughter of Ann Boleyn.

Criterion materials

Five free-writing exercises constituted the criterion materials. Two were essays with a total time allowance of 40 minutes each, and three were hardly more than extended paragraphs—each to be done in 20 minutes. The total amount of free writing required was, therefore, that which could be done in two hours and 20 minutes, divided into two full class periods and three half-class periods, assuming that there were 40 minutes per period.

The shorter essays were designed to elicit immediate or very prompt responses; in fact, two of the three assignments ended with a suggestion for a first sentence. The longer essays were based upon more complex and detailed situations requiring analysis and some decision regarding interpretation, point of view, or a judgment that was to be stated and supported. Directions for these essays suggested making plans and notes prior to writing and advised students to use about 10 minutes for planning and about 30 minutes for actual writing.

The subject matter of the essays was devised with some hope of stimulating different "types" of writing, once called forms of discourse—descriptive, narrative, expository, and argumentative writing. One short essay was aimed at the description of an interesting element in the student's home town, as told to a foreign student in a pen pal letter. Another essay required the student to write in narrative form an imaginative story about an experience (as participant or observer) or about a commonplace inanimate object. The topic of the third essay suggested that teen-age students are much more conventional than their elders and required an exposition, with reasons supporting or attacking the idea. The two longer essays were both "expository-argumentative," with the analysis of a situation or a character as the point of departure for the expression of an opinion. One emphasized opinion, producing what the books call argumentative discourse, by requiring the student to decide upon and defend a course of action toward an errant student. (The student, secretary-treasurer of the student body, has neglected his duties.) The other long essay called for a character analysis based

on the brief talk of a college freshman given to the
student body of his high school alma mater. Because
the talk had to do with the freshman's ideas about
college, the resulting essays might (and usually did)
elicit arguments, or statements about the writers'
opinions, in addition to the exposition that was based
on the required analysis of the speaker's character.

The testing population and the sample

All the measuring instruments described above (six
20-minute objective tests or test sections, two interlinear exercises, and five free-writing exercises) were
administered to one class of eleventh-grade and one
of twelfth-grade students of English in each of 24
secondary schools. The schools were all member in-
stitutions of the College Entrance Examination
Board. They represented both public and independent schools of various sizes in cities and smaller com-
munities, and in all commonly listed major geo-
graphical areas of the country. (A listing of these
schools will be found in Appendix A.) Classes averaged about 27 students enrolled, or 55 students per
school, for a total population of more than 1,300.

In seeking the cooperation of the schools, it was
requested that classes of average ability and achievement be selected. This was done to avoid the possibility of a limited range of testing results. It was assumed that a maximum spread of abilities would be
needed to produce meaningful results from a relatively small number of students, from tests of limited
length (that is, actual test sections, most of which required 20 minutes, yet nevertheless were supposed

to produce reliable scores), and from an as yet un-
proved free-writing criterion. The assumption was
proved to be only partly accurate. Meaningful results
were later obtained from scores on the tests taken by
parts of the sample intentionally restricted to one
grade and restricted to those students with an evi-
dent intention or desire to attend a College Board
member college.

Complete data were obtained for 646 cases, approximately half of whom were enrolled in grade 11
and half in grade 12. Of these, 533 had taken the
PSAT and 158 took the SAT prior to the analysis of the
data.

Procedure

a. *Testing.* The tests, including interlinear exercises and essays, were administered in the fall of 1961
under standard testing conditions by classroom
teachers or, in one or two instances, by or under the
direction of supervisors of testing or guidance direc-
tors. It was suggested, but not required, that the
regular time of the classes be used for the purpose.
Schedules were at the option of teachers or school
administrators, provided only that testing be completed prior to the Thanksgiving holiday of the
school and that at least one day intervene between
testing dates. A normal schedule assumed that testing would be done during three weeks in late October
and in November, at the convenience of the school,
and that classes two days a week, or three days maximum (Monday, Wednesday, and Friday), would be
devoted to this purpose. The sequence of tests pre-

scribed also separated the interlinears from the essay exercises to the greatest extent possible. It was suggested that the teachers take some time in class prior to the day of the first test to explain the project, emphasizing its value to the student as practice in test-taking and in extemporaneous free writing under testing conditions. Further motivation was stimulated by the offer to furnish each school the approximate scores of its pupils on a College Board English Composition Test. (This was to be done by using the sum of scores of three separated test sections all of which were originally parts of a single final form, and converting these total raw scores to the Board scale by using the original formula.)

b. *Scoring the tests.* The objective tests and interlinear exercises were scored according to standard procedures. The two interlinear exercises were scored by 25 experienced readers under the direction of the chief reader for the English Composition Test. The original rubrics and scoring manuals were reprinted with very minor changes and used by the readers. The scores on the six 20-minute objective tests and on the two interlinear exercises constituted the set of eight variables to be correlated separately and in various combinations with the criterion scores.

c. *Scoring the essays.* Readers of the interlinear exercises were also used for reading and scoring the criterion essays; in fact, all of the reading was done in a single five-day session. It should be noted that the readers had had no experience in reading brief extemporaneous essays produced by average elev-

enth- and twelfth-grade students. Some had read essays written for the College Board Advanced Placement Examination in English under directions requiring analytical reading.

The readers were asked to make global or holistic, not analytical, judgments of each paper, reading rapidly for a total impression. There were only three ratings: a score of "3" for a superior paper, "2" for an average paper, and "1" for an inferior paper. The readers were told to judge each paper on its merits without regard to other papers on the same topic; that is, they were not to be concerned with any idea of a normal distribution of the three scores. They were advised that scores of "3" were possible and that the "safe" procedure of awarding almost all "2s" was to be avoided. Standards for the ratings were established in two ways: by furnishing each reader with copies of the sample essays for inspection and discussion, and by explaining the conditions of administration and the nature of the testing population; and by having all readers score reproduced sets of carefully selected sample answers to all five questions and to report the results. The scores were then tabulated and announced. No effort was made to identify any reader whose standards were out of line, because that fact would be known to him and would be assumed to have a corrective effect. The procedure was repeated several times during the first two days of scoring to assist readers in maintaining standards.

Each essay was scored independently by five different readers. The essays of each student were so distributed and redistributed that all 25 readers would score at least one essay produced by each student. The procedure worked well in general, but differences in reading speed eventually had the result of limiting to 22 or 23 the number of different readers who scored the papers of a few students. Because there were five scores for each essay ranging from a possible five "1s" to a possible five "3s," the scores on each essay could range from 5 to 15, and on each set of five essays produced by a student the scores had a possible range of 25 to 75.

3. The criterion

An analysis of the grades assigned to the 646 papers by the 25 readers revealed that our expectations were more than met. The means, standard deviations, and intercorrelations of the 25 sets of scores are recorded in Table I of Appendix B. Summaries and statistical treatment of the data appear in Tables 1, 2, 3, and 4.

In Table 1 are details of an analysis of variance of the ratings. The reading reliability is estimated by dividing the mean square for students minus the mean square for error by the mean square for students. The result is a correlation coefficient of .921. This means that if a second group of 25 readers as competent as the first group were chosen and the papers were read again, it might be expected that the two sets of total scores would produce a correlation of approximately .921. Score reliability is estimated by using the mean square for the interaction of students and topics as the error term. This is because the score reliability is an estimate of the correlation

Table 1: Analysis of variance of the essay reading and estimates of reading reliability and of test reliability of total essay score

Source of variation	Degree of freedom	Sum of squares	Mean square	
Students	645	2167.878	3.3611**	
Topics	4	188.535	47.1338**	
Readings	4	47.575	11.8938**	
Students x topic	2580	1377.785	.5340**	
Students x readings	2580	686.745	.2662	⎫
Topics x readings	16	10.122	.6336**	⎬ .266
Error	10320	2735.588	.2651	⎭
Total	16149	7214.198		

** Significant at 1 percent level

$$\frac{3.3611 - .2651}{3.3611} = .921 \text{ Reliability of reading}$$

$$\frac{3.3611 - .5340}{3.3611} = .841 \text{ Reliability of total essay score}$$

to be expected if the students were to write five more essays on five new topics and if these essays were read by 25 new readers. The estimate of the correlation between the sums of this second set of ratings and the original sums is .841.

There are other figures of interest in the analysis of variance table. The mean square for topics is significant, indicating that the ratings assigned varied from topic to topic. When the score is the sum of such ratings, one does not need to be concerned about such differences. The differences are significant, however, under certain other conditions. For example, if the five topics had been assigned as alternate topics from which one or two could be chosen by students, a student's rating might depend more on which topic he chose than on how well he wrote. Or if one topic had been assigned to one form of a test and another topic to a second form, then some method of equating the scores would be required; otherwise, the magnitude of an individual's score would depend partly on which form of the test he wrote. Differences among the difficulties of the topics would be part of the error.

The mean square for readings is also significant, indicating that scores were higher or lower for some of the five readings than they were for others. Again, these differences are of no particular concern when the score is the total of all the readings. But suppose that thousands of papers had been read and that some had been read early and others late in the reading period of several days. Then a student's score might have depended on when in the period his paper happened to be read as well as on how well he wrote.

Some idea of the magnitude of the differences across topics and across readings can be gained by studying Table 2. The average total score on topic C (Imagine) was 9.61 while that for topic E (STEP 2D) was only 8.22. The two topics cannot be used interchangeably without an adjustment for differences in inherent difficulty. Most of the differences from reading to reading arise from the difference between the average for the first reading (9.16) and those for the other four readings (8.64, 8.53, 8.70, and 8.36). Apparently the readers were more generous during the early part of the reading period than later. In reading a large number of papers, it might be wise to have the readers continue practice readings until it has been determined that they have reached an acceptable level of agreement. To begin actual scoring of papers too soon might give a special advantage to those whose papers were read during the first few hours.

The significant student-by-topic interaction has already been mentioned in connection with the estimation of the score reliability. It is interpreted as indicating that some of the students do relatively better on some topics while other students do relatively better on other topics. Could this problem not be overcome by offering the students alternate topics? Unfortunately not. In the first place, there is no evidence that the average student is able to judge which topic will give him the advantage. In the second place, the variability in topics already discussed would be introducing error at the same time that students might be eliminating error by choosing the

Table 2: Means and standard deviations of scores on the five readings of each of five essay topics
(*N = 646*)

Topic		Reading order					Total score
		First	Second	Third	Fourth	Fifth	
A. Pen pal	—Mean	1.87	1.76	1.79	1.82	1.70	8.95
	S.D.	.69	.65	.64	.64	.65	2.26
B. Teen-ager	—Mean	1.68	1.60	1.62	1.63	1.58	8.12
	S.D.	.69	.64	.67	.66	.65	2.42
C. Imagine	—Mean	2.03	1.87	1.86	1.87	1.78	9.41
	S.D.	.70	.65	.66	.66	.66	2.39
D. STEP 2C	—Mean	1.88	1.81	1.71	1.81	1.73	8.93
	S.D.	.68	.65	.66	.64	.65	2.30
E. STEP 2D	—Mean	1.70	1.60	1.55	1.57	1.57	7.99
	S.D.	.67	.64	.63	.62	.63	2.32
Total	—Mean	9.16	8.64	8.53	8.70	8.36	43.40
	S.D.	2.26	2.10	2.05	2.03	2.06	9.16

topic on which they were most adequately prepared.

The particular design used in this experiment does not permit one to estimate the variance among readers, an important source of error in any operational reading. Here every reader contributed to the total score for each student so that any difference in standards from reader to reader was eliminated. But in a situation where one reader rated the papers of some students while another reader rated those of other students, any differences in standards would contribute to error.

It might appear from the discussion thus far that obtaining a reliable essay score in any large-scale reading is difficult if not impossible. On the other hand, as will be demonstrated later, even relatively unreliable essay scores in combination with other types of questions can be useful. A careful consideration of the various sources of error revealed by the analysis of variance can serve as a guide to the design of an operational reading.

The large variance across topics indicates that no options should be permitted; each student should write on every topic presented. The undoubted presence of variance among readers can be minimized by having several different readers contribute to whatever score is developed. Instead of worrying about ways of increasing the reliability of single readings, the use of multiple readings is recommended. These readings should be distributed throughout the reading period since there seems to be a significant variance associated with the time sequence. Finally, unless some equating procedure is developed, there is no assurance that essay scores developed from one test are equivalent to scores from another.

Table 3: *Average correlations between single readings within essay topics and across essay topics*

Topic	A	B	C	D	E
A. Pen pal	.366				
B. Teen-ager	.237	.411			
C. Imagine	.242	.261	.385		
D. STEP 2C	.253	.264	.260	.361	
E. STEP 2D	.221	.308	.269	.297	.408
T. Total essay score	.518*	.574*	.554*	.561*	.581*

* Spuriously high because part is included in the total.

Table 4: *Correlations between total scores on the five readings of each essay topic (estimates of reading reliabilities are shown in parentheses)*
($N = 646$)

Topic	A	B	C	D	E	Total
A. Pen pal	(.743)					
B. Teen-ager	.466	(.777)				
C. Imagine	.483	.505	(.758)			
D. STEP 2C	.516	.521	.523	(.739)		
E. STEP 2D	.435	.584	.520	.592	(.775)	
T. Total essay score	.738*	.791*	.777*	.804*	.800*	(.921)

* Spuriously high because part is included in the total.

15

The analysis of variance provides the basic data for estimating reliability of scores based on any number of topics and any number of readings; however, estimates can also be obtained for certain combinations from the intercorrelations among readings of a single topic and those among readings of different topics. Averages of such correlations based on single readings are presented in Table 3; those based on five readings can be found in Table 4. The diagonal entries in each table are estimates of reading reliabilities; the other entries are estimates of score reliabilities. Score reliabilities for single topics read once range from .221 to .308. Reading reliabilities for single topics read once range from .361 to .411. There is no evidence that greater reliability is achieved with the two 40-minute exercises (topics D and E), than for the three 20-minute essays.

When scores are the sums of five readings, score reliabilities range from .435 to .592 and reading reliabilities from .739 to .777. These are not significantly different from reliabilities previously reported. The singularity of these data consists in the fact that the total score on all five essays is highly reliable and can serve as a sound criterion for evaluating the various types of questions in the English Composition Test.

4. Relations between predictors and the criterion

Data based on total sample

The criterion having been established, it is now possible to examine the relative validity of the several subtests. In Table 5 are presented the correlations of the subtest scores not only with the total essay scores but also with the total scores on each of the five essays.

The validity coefficients of greatest interest are those in the last column of the table. The least valid test is subtest 1, paragraph organization. Coefficients for the seven remaining subtests range from .568 for prose groups to .705 for sentence correction and .707

for usage. Even the correlations with individual essays are substantial. The mean correlation of subtest 1 with the five essays is .359, and for the other subtests, in order, the means are .553, .551, .444, .463, .504, .522, and .504. In view of these figures it appears that the objective form of the College Board English Composition Test is composed of highly valid item types.

Any combination of three subtests selected from tests 1 to 6 constitutes a one-hour examination. The correlation of the sum of the raw scores with the criterion, T, is an estimate of the validity of the total one-hour test. Of the 20 possible combinations of three subtests, some would not normally be used in practice. For example, usage and sentence correction are so similar that it is not likely that both would be

Table 5: Correlations of English Composition Test subtest scores with the sum of five scores on each essay and with the total essay score

$(N = 646)$

Subtest	Pen pal A	Teen-ager B	Imagine C	STEP 2C D	STEP 2D E	Total essay T
1. Paragraph organization	.335	.347	.352	.388	.372	.458
2. Usage	.535	.541	.538	.577	.575	.707
3. Sentence correction	.503	.545	.550	.574	.585	.705
4. Prose groups	.399	.465	.426	.466	.462	.568
5. Error recognition	.403	.455	.443	.517	.498	.592
6. Construction shift	.436	.521	.503	.530	.531	.645
7. Interlinear (Valley Forge)	.454	.524	.503	.571	.560	.668
8. Interlinear (housefly)	.473	.483	.493	.543	.527	.644

included in the same test. On the other hand, both have long been regarded as such satisfactory item types that every one of the several recent forms of the English Composition Test has contained one or the other. Twelve of the 20 possible combinations contain either test 2 or 3 but not both. The correlations of their raw-score sums with the criterion are given in the left-hand section of Table 6.

The validity coefficients for the 12 combinations range from .717 for tests 1, 3, and 4 to .748 for tests 2, 4, and 5 and for tests 2, 4, and 6. Coefficients for combinations that include test 1 are all below .73, whereas those without test 1 are .74 or higher.

The first five combinations in the first column have been used in recent operational forms of the English Composition Test. Even the least valid combination, the first one listed in the table, has a higher validity coefficient than any that has previously been reported for the English Composition Test, not, it is believed, because current forms of the test are more

Table 6: Validity of selected combinations of subtest scores
(N = 646)
(Tests 1-6: 20 minutes, objective. Tests 7, 8: 30 minutes, interlinear)

60-minute examination		70-minute examination				50-minute examination	
Tests	Validity	Tests	Validity	Tests	Validity	Tests	Validity
1,3,4	.717	1,3,7	.737	1,3,8	.735	1,7	.669
1,3,5	.723	1,4,7	.711	1,4,8	.706	1,8	.655
2,4,6	.748	1,5,7	.718	1,5,8	.716	2,7	.743
2,5,6	.744	2,4,7	.757	2,4,8	.765	2,8	.755
3,4,5	.740	2,5,7	.754	2,5,8	.764	3,7	.747
1,2,4	.723	2,6,7	.757	2,6,8	.767	3,8	.747
1,2,5	.725	3,4,7	.758	3,4,8	.759	4,7	.710
1,2,6	.728	3,5,7	.759	3,5,8	.763	4,8	.704
1,3,6	.720	4,5,7	.737	4,5,8	.738	5,7	.715
2,4,5	.748	4,6,7	.740	4,6,8	.739	5,8	.714
3,4,6	.741	5,6,7	.740	5,6,8	.743	6,7	.722
3,5,6	.742					6,8	.717

valid than earlier forms but because the criterion is a far better assessment of writing ability than are such measures as school marks or teachers' ratings, which have been used in the past.

In order to investigate the validity of the interlinear exercise, consider the first five combinations and replace one of the subtests by one of the interlinears, tests 7 and 8. These particular sets produce 11 different pairs, to be combined with an interlinear. The results are listed in the middle section of Table 6. The new validity estimate is higher than the original one when test 7 or test 8 is substituted for test 1, 4, 5, or 6 and lower when substituted for test 2 or test 3. The increases tend to exceed the decreases. Since test 2 or test 3 is likely to be retained in any event, the decreases may be regarded as irrelevant from a practical point of view.

The right-hand section of Table 6 shows that even the simple combination of an interlinear exercise and one objective test produces a validity estimate that exceeds .70 for every combination except those involving the least valid subtest, test 1. It may be of incidental interest that the sum of raw scores on test 2 and 3 has a correlation of .749 with the criterion, a finding that strongly suggests that the characteristics of single sentences play an important part in the overall impression made on the reader. The highest correlation obtained (.775) was for a combination of three subtests which included both test 2 and test 3.

Validities involving a verbal score

It was found that 533 of the 646 examinees had PSAT scores on file at ETS. Of the 533 students with PSAT scores, 262 were juniors who had taken the PSAT shortly before the experimental testing, and 211 were seniors who had taken it the previous year when they

Table 7: Subgroup means and standard deviations

Subgroup	1	2	3	4	5	6	7	8	T	PSAT-V	SAT-V
262 Juniors											
Mean	11.30	24.33	27.28	10.60	18.21	17.58	27.22	22.95	43.78	48.5	
S.D.	5.83	8.06	7.43	6.40	5.97	5.36	6.74	6.49	8.49	9.5	
211 Seniors											
Mean	13.42	26.72	29.43	11.76	18.33	18.35	29.20	25.24	46.42	46.8	
S.D.	6.35	7.81	7.11	6.48	6.09	5.26	6.59	7.14	8.79	10.2	
158 Cases with SAT											
Mean	14.27	27.12	29.91	12.59	18.12	19.03	29.44	25.94	46.80	..	508
S.D.	6.37	8.12	7.00	6.59	6.57	5.53	6.97	7.04	8.99	..	104

were juniors. The 60 remaining students who took the PSAT in their senior year are not included here. There is also a group of 158 students for whom there are SAT scores on file. This latter group partially overlaps the junior and senior PSAT groups.

Complete tables of correlations for the three subgroups are included in Appendix B. Reproduced in Table 7 are means and standard deviations of the subtests, the criterion, and the verbal scores.

From the PSAT means it appears that the senior group were slightly less successful with the verbal

material when they were juniors than the junior group, but the difference is not great. All the subtest means show an increase—an indication of growth—from the junior to the senior level. The highest means, for the most part, occur for the group with SAT scores. Contrary to expectation, however, this group shows no tendency to be more homogeneous than the junior and senior groups, possibly because it contains both juniors and seniors. All three subgroups tend to be less variable than the original total group, but the differences are small, so that validity

Table 8: Validity estimates of selected sums (X) of subtest scores and of best weighted combinations of X and PSAT-*verbal or* SAT-*verbal scores*

Subtests (X)	Juniors (N = 262) $r_{TV} = .641$		Seniors (N = 211) $r_{TV} = .697$		SAT Group (N = 158) $r_{TV} = .632$	
	r_{TX}	$R_{T.XV}$	r_{TX}	$R_{T.XV}$	r_{TX}	$R_{T.X}$
1,3,6	.651	.707	.696	.746	.676	.704
1,3,7	.671	.718	.715	.749	.717	.726
1,3,8	.674	.719	.698	.745	.673	.699
2,4,6	.709	.733	.711	.754	.686	.707
2,5,6	.692	.723	.702	.748	.689	.706
2,6,7	.708	.740	.717	.755	.719	.729
2,6,8	.722	.747	.711	.754	.690	.709
3,4,6	.695	.723	.714	.754	.687	.707
3,5,6	.679	.714	.711	.750	.699	.710
3,6,7	.699	.733	.724	.757	.725	.732
3,6,8	.705	.735	.705	.751	.683	.705

coefficients based on the subgroups may be expected to be only slightly lower than those based on the total group.

Some typical coefficients have been selected for presentation in order to demonstrate the general order of magnitude of the findings. In Table 8 are listed data for 11 combinations of subtests. Each combination, X, is the sum of the raw scores on the subtests indicated.

In each section heading the correlation of the appropriate verbal score with the criterion, T, is given. These are .641 for juniors, .697 for seniors, and .632 for the group with SAT scores. Not included in the table are values of r_{XV}, which range from .671 to .726 for juniors, from .742 to .777 for seniors, and from .742 to .792 for the SAT group. Note that in the body of the table there is only one value of r_{TX} as low as the corresponding r_{TV}. Although the verbal scores on both the PSAT and the SAT are good predictors of the criterion, the traditional English Composition Test is better.

The multiple correlations, $R_{T.XV}$, show the substantial gain in validity that can be achieved when the verbal measure is used in conjunction with the English Composition Test. Where r_{TX} ranges from .651 to .725, the range of $R_{T.XV}$ is from .699 to .757.

Throughout the table the coefficients involving test 7 or test 8 tend to be higher than those where no interlinear exercise is included. Although the differences are small, the data show that the interlinear at least holds its own among other exercises and appears to make a unique contribution to the validity of any English Composition Test of which it is a part.

Validities in relation to level of ability

It is generally conceded that objective, machine-scorable questions can be used to measure a student's mastery of the elements of correct writing, that is, of the rules of grammar, usage, punctuation, and spelling. It is a relatively simple task to develop a series of sentences and to ask the student to identify those which are correct and those which contain errors—particularly if the errors identify the writer as unschooled or careless. But, it is argued, there is more to effective writing than the avoidance of gross errors. One has to be able to organize sentences and paragraphs into an effective whole. The truly effective writer has developed an individual style. He not only avoids errors: he also communicates ideas and moves the reader to feel intensely or to act in relation to the ideas which are communicated. If the College Board English Composition Test is to be an acceptable test of writing ability, it needs to differentiate beyond the pedestrian level of simple mechanics.

We have demonstrated that the one-hour English Composition Test does an amazingly effective job of ordering students in the same way as a trained group of readers would after reading a sizable sample of their actual writing. With the possible exception of paragraph organization, all the types of items used in the test appear to have acceptable validity. The interlinear exercise is apparently making a special contribution to validity. On the other hand, this special contribution appears to be relatively small when one considers the additional cost of including the interlinear in a test. Is it possible, however, that the analysis of data based on total groups has failed to tell the whole story? Is it possible that the interlinear exercise is making its primary contribution in assessing ability among students who have mastered the mechanics of writing? What would be the relative validity of the interlinear exercise for a group of students who stand relatively high on the fundamentals as measured by one of the more routine machine-scorable item types, for example, usage?

To answer these questions a special study was conducted using four groups of students, two with high scores on usage and two with low scores on usage. The samples consist of the 211 seniors and the 262 juniors for whom junior year PSAT scores were available. Each of these groups was divided into a high and a low group on the basis of scores on the usage subtest, and the intercorrelations of the various measures were determined. The correlation tables for the four samples are Tables VI, VII, VIII, and IX in Appendix B.

The means and standard deviations on the several measures are brought together in Table 9. As would be expected, the high and low groups differ most markedly on the measure used to make the divisions,

Table 9: Means and standard deviations for senior and junior groups scoring high and low on "usage"

Subgroup	1	2[a]	3	4	5	6	7	8	T	PSAT-V
131 Low juniors										
Mean	9.15	17.69	22.94	8.01	15.31	14.80	23.31	20.06	39.11	43.4
S. D.	5.11	5.17	6.79	5.42	5.76	5.02	5.44	6.01	6.53	8.2
131 High juniors										
Mean	13.45	30.96	31.63	13.18	21.11	20.36	31.12	25.85	48.45	53.5
S.D.	5.72	3.91	5.15	6.26	4.63	4.10	5.55	5.60	7.61	7.8
106 Low seniors										
Mean	11.53	20.22	25.21	8.73	15.22	15.25	25.33	21.86	42.30	41.4
S.D.	5.33	4.32	6.34	5.34	5.20	4.43	5.62	6.17	7.43	7.9
105 High seniors										
Mean	15.33	33.29	33.70	14.83	21.48	21.48	33.11	28.66	50.58	52.2
S.D.	6.71	4.25	4.98	6.08	5.24	4.05	5.00	6.38	8.07	9.3

a. The senior group and the junior group were each divided into "high" and "low" subgroups on the basis of their scores on subtest 2, usage.

he usage subtest. But they also differ significantly on all the other measures. The mean PSAT scores are approximately 10 points apart (equivalent to 100 points on the College Board scale). It should be remembered that the PSAT scores for both juniors and seniors were obtained in October of the junior year. Thus, although the senior group is slightly less able than the junior group, there has been an additional year of intellectual growth. It is not surprising, therefore, that the seniors make higher scores on all the measures of writing ability. It may be instructive to compare the figures in Table 9 with those in Table 7 where the data for the total groups of seniors and juniors are reported.

The validity coefficients for the several measures are reported in Table 10. Perhaps the most striking element of this table is the relatively high validity for the usage score even after the subtest was used as the basis for dividing the groups. But there are other points of interest. Seven of the nine coefficients for the high seniors (column four) are higher than the corresponding coefficients for the low seniors (column three). These seven include the ones based on the PSAT-verbal score and one of the interlinear exercises. The other interlinear exercise and the sentence correction subtest are more valid for the low seniors. For the juniors, the picture is reversed. Eight of the nine comparisons of corresponding columns of figures favor the low juniors, and the one which favors the high juniors is that based on the same interlinear

Table 10: Correlations of English Composition Test subtest scores and PSAT-verbal scores with total essay score for junior and senior groups scoring low and high on "usage"

Variable	Low juniors N = 131	High juniors N = 131	Low seniors N = 106	High seniors N = 105
1. Paragraph organization	.233	.209	.346	.443
2. Usage[a]	.488	.412	.462	.556
3. Sentence correction	.539	.492	.601	.451
4. Prose groups	.406	.341	.451	.467
5. Error recognition	.402	.235	.359	.510
6. Construction shift	.526	.301	.378	.559
7. Interlinear (Valley Forge)	.412	.354	.493	.560
8. Interlinear (housefly)	.379	.443	.488	.475
9. PSAT-verbal	.540	.451	.509	.670

a. Groups were divided on the basis of scores on subtest 2, usage.

exercise which was more valid for the low seniors.

On the basis of the simple correlation coefficients in Table 10, it is impossible to establish any differential pattern for the interlinear exercise. Fluctuations from sample to sample are likely to be as great between two different interlinear exercises as they are among the different item types. But the central interest is not in isolated item types but rather in one-hour English Composition Tests made up of several item types. The basic question to be answered for any sample is this: What is the relative validity of a one-hour English Composition Test containing an interlinear exercise and one which is completely machine-scorable when both are combined with a verbal aptitude test and the criterion is a reliable score on a representative sample of actual writing?

In Table 11 are assembled typical coefficients based on the sums of three subtests and on the best weighted combinations of these sums and PSAT-verbal scores. The organization of this table is similar to that of Table 8, except that subtests 1 and 2 are not included in the combinations. The first four rows of Table 11 present coefficients based on all-objective combinations; the means of the four rows are presented in line five. Coefficients based on combinations which include an interlinear exercise follow, and the final line contains the means of these coefficients.

The data offer little support for the hypothesis that the interlinear exercise is most effective for predicting the writing ability of students who have mastered writing mechanics. The means of the coeffi-

cients based on the one-hour combinations of all-objective questions are .582, .475, .603, and .608 for the low and high juniors and the low and high seniors respectively. The comparable coefficients for the combinations which include an interlinear exercise are .569, .507, .611, and .628. For the two samples of juniors, there is an average difference of .045 in favor of the hypothesis, that is, .507 + .582 is .045 greater than .475 + .569. For the samples of seniors the corresponding difference is .028, that is, .628 + .603 is .028 greater than .608 + .611. But when the PSAT-verbal scores are included, the average difference drops to .038 for the juniors and to .001 for the seniors. (See Table 11.) For the samples of seniors, combinations which include an interlinear score produce, on the average, higher coefficients for both high and low groups.

In general, the data presented here are consistent with those presented in previous sections of this chapter. The several objective types of questions are valid for predicting a reliable criterion of writing ability. A one-hour English Composition Test made up of three different types of questions when combined with the verbal section of the PSAT or the SAT produces a multiple correlation coefficient which is very high by the usual standards against which validity coefficients are judged. The interlinear exercise is one of the more valid types of question and often contributes uniquely to the multiple correlation. There is no convincing evidence that a particular type of question is more appropriate than any other for measuring the writing ability of students who

Table 11: *Validity estimates of sums (X) of subtest scores and of best weighted combinations of X and* PSAT-*verbal scores for high and low groups*

Subtests (X)	Low juniors $r_{TV} = .540$ $N = 131$		High juniors $r_{TV} = .450$ $N = 131$		Low seniors $r_{TV} = .509$ $N = 106$		High seniors $r_{TV} = .670$ $N = 105$	
	r_{TX}	$R_{T.XV}$	r_{TX}	$R_{T.XV}$	r_{TX}	$R_{T.XV}$	r_{TX}	$R_{T.XV}$
3,4,5	.574	.607	.503	.545	.635	.648	.596	.691
3,4,6	.593	.620	.517	.566	.634	.652	.586	.697
3,5,6	.595	.628	.453	.524	.588	.616	.625	.706
4,5,6	.565	.603	.427	.515	.556	.603	.624	.708
Mean of 4 coefficients	.582	.615	.475	.537	.603	.630	.608	.700
3,4,7	.570	.611	.547	.586	.670	.677	.616	.694
3,5,7	.572	.620	.504	.553	.638	.648	.641	.699
3,6,7	.589	.631	.508	.570	.619	.639	.639	.708
4,5,7	.537	.594	.462	.535	.610	.632	.654	.705
4,6,7	.559	.607	.483	.559	.605	.634	.651	.713
5,6,7	.569	.620	.428	.524	.552	.597	.673	.721
3,4,8	.573	.602	.587	.621	.654	.664	.587	.693
3,5,8	.581	.613	.544	.587	.629	.640	.609	.698
3,6,8	.593	.622	.543	.602	.607	.630	.591	.703
4,5,8	.546	.585	.500	.556	.601	.624	.632	.705
4,6,8	.562	.596	.516	.589	.593	.625	.614	.709
5,6,8	.579	.612	.462	.553	.550	.594	.634	.715
Mean of 12 coefficients	.569	.609	.507	.570	.611	.634	.638	.705

score high on a test of knowledge of writing mechanics.

Validity of an English Composition Test that includes an essay

As these computations were in progress, a new idea took shape, namely, that a form of the English Composition Test consisting of two 20-minute objective subtests and a 20-minute essay might be worth considering. Although the original study was not planned with this possibility in mind, it was felt that the present data could be used to provide a preliminary answer to the question of the feasibility of such an examination and that, if preliminary findings should be favorable, further study would be indicated.

The present data include three 20-minute essays: A, pen pal; B, teen-ager; and C, imagine. If one of these essays is used as a predictor variable, it can not also remain in the criterion. Therefore, for present purposes, a four-essay criterion will be used, which, of course, is somewhat less reliable than the original criterion, T. Lest the validity coefficients based on one of these essays turn out to be atypical in some respect and so lead to unwarranted conclusions, coefficients based on each of the three in turn have been computed. Thus, when essay A is a predictor variable, the new criterion, the sum of essays B, C, D, and E, will be denoted T_A; that is, the original criterion with A removed.

The samples to be used in this investigation are the junior and senior samples with PSAT-verbal scores (Tables IV and V in Appendix B). The reliability of the criterion scores can be estimated if the four essays are treated as parallel subtests. Because they are not truly parallel, the resulting estimates may properly be regarded as lower bounds. They are:

	Juniors	Seniors
T_A	.810	.781
T_B	.781	.760
T_C	.801	.763

Results of a few of the many possible combinations of subtests are given in Table 12. The first line of the table deals with the objective subtests 1 and 2, the interlinear subtest 7, and the PSAT-verbal. The best weighted sum of these four variables has a correlation of .728 with T_A for the junior subgroup and one of .745 for the senior subgroup. In the second line the interlinear exercise has been replaced by essay A, and the multiple correlations increase from .728 to .744 for juniors and from .745 to .756 for seniors. The table contains nine such comparisons for juniors and nine for seniors, and in every instance the essay contributes more to the prediction than does the interlinear exercise. The multiple correlations differ only a little from the estimated reliabilities of the criteria.

In practice it is easier to use simple sums of raw scores or, possibly, to use integral multipliers, than it is to apply the actual regression weights, which are "best" only for the group for which they were computed, in any case. Since the essay variables consistently have substantial beta-weights and at the same time relatively small raw-score standard de-

Table 12: Multiple correlations for selected sets of predictors

Four predictors			Two predictors		
Variables	Juniors	Seniors	Variables	Juniors	Seniors
Criterion = T_A:					
1,2,7,V	.728	.745			
1,2,A,V	.744	.756	(1+2+4A), V	.738	.754
2,6,8,V	.741	.743			
2,6,A,V	.757	.761	(2+6+4A), V	.756	.760
3,4,7,V	.734	.757			
3,4,A,V	.754	.766	(3+4+4A), V	.746	.766
Criterion = T_B:					
1,2,7,V	.740	.732			
1,2,B,V	.796	.758	(1+2+4B), V	.781	.753
2,6,8,V	.747	.742			
2,6,B,V	.796	.767	(2+6+4B), V	.789	.767
3,4,7,V	.738	.739			
3,4,B,V	.792	.761	(3+4+4B), V	.784	.758
Criterion = T_C:					
1,2,7,V	.719	.738			
1,2,C,V	.747	.760	(1+2+4C), V	.729	.758
2,6,8,V	.736	.734			
2,6,C,V	.754	.761	(2+6+4C), V	.753	.760
3,4,7,V	.712	.747			
3,4,C,V	.733	.766	(3+4+4C), V	.731	.764

viations, a reasonable raw-score combination for the present data appears to be the sum of the two objective-section scores plus four times the essay score. The effect of such a sum is to give the essay score about 25 percent more weight than either of the objective scores. Data for such combinations are presented in the right-hand portion of Table 12. In most cases the loss in the multiple correlation is negligible. It is similar to the shrinkage found when a regression equation based on one group is applied to scores made by a parallel group. Of particular interest is the fact that each of these 18 values remains higher than that for the four-predictor equation where the interlinear exercise is one of the variables.

5. The field trial

The experimental study reported in the preceding chapters established the fact that five of the six types of multiple-choice questions used in the English Composition Test are remarkably effective for predicting scores on a reliable criterion of writing ability. It also demonstrated that combinations of subtests which include an interlinear exercise tend to be slightly more valid than combinations which include only multiple-choice questions; in other words, the interlinear exercise makes a singular contribution to the prediction of writing ability. Finally, the study strongly suggested that the highest validity would be obtained if a 20-minute essay were included in the test.

There were, however, a number of questions which needed to be answered before a decision to use an essay in an operational test could be justified. In the experimental study, the predictor essays had been read by the same group of 25 highly qualified readers who had read the criterion essays, and both criterion and predictor essays had been read in the same reading session. The readings of the criterion and predictor essays were not so independent as one would wish for an ideal validity study. Furthermore, in any operational setting it would be necessary to use hundreds of readers, many of whom would necessarily be less experienced than the readers in the experimental study and all of whom would have to continue reading essays on a single topic for four or five days. The readers in the original study alternated among five topics. To what extent could comparable results be achieved by a cross section of the many readers working under operational conditions?

Furthermore, the predictor essays had been read by five different readers. The data suggested that three readings of an essay could be completed in about the same time required to read an interlinear exercise. The cost of reading would be roughly proportional to the number of readings. Would the essay continue to make a distinctive contribution to validity if scores were based on fewer than five readings? Assuming that both reliability of reading and correlations with the criterion might be lower for an operational reading, how many readings would be required to insure that the essay would make a unique contribution to validity?

We also wished to explore the possibility that a four-point scale might be more effective than the three-point scale used in reading essays in the experimental study. There had been some evidence that readers tended to use the middle category whenever there was any doubt, thus restricting the variance of essay scores. The employment of a four-point scale would force a choice of one or the other side of the midpoint of the scale and should increase the reliability of the reading. Would there be any increase in efficiency if a four-point rather than a three-point scale were used? Or would any increase in reliability and validity be accompanied by a comparable reduction in reading rate? The study reported in this chapter was designed to provide data for answering these questions.

In this study we wished to compare essay reading under operational conditions with the reading carried out in the original experiment. The sample for the study consists of the 533 cases from the original study for whom PSAT scores are available. The 145 readers who had assembled to grade the interlinear exercise included in the December 1962 form of the English Composition Test spent part of one day preparing for and carrying out the field-trial reading. The essay papers for topic A and for topic B (both 20-minute topics) were read according to the design outlined in Table 13.

The 533 papers for topic A were divided into nine packs and those for topic B into eight packs. Thus there were 17 packs of papers, corresponding to the 17 tables set up for the interlinear reading. Five packs of essays on topic A were read on a three-point scale at tables 1, 2, 3, 4, and 5 (sample A-3). The design called for these papers to be read five times, once at each of the tables. Four packs of essays on topic B were read four times each on a three-point scale at tables 6, 7, 8, and 9 (sample B-3). The readers at tables 10, 11, 12, and 13 read four packs of essays on topic A four times each on a four-point scale; and readers at tables 14, 15, 16, and 17 read four packs of papers on topic B four times each on a four-point scale (samples A-4 and B-4). Because readers did not have access to the scores assigned by previous readers, each score was assigned independently.

The following variables have been included in a correlation matrix for each of the four samples:

1. First field-trial reading (topic A or topic B, depending on the sample)
2. Second field-trial reading
3. Third field-trial reading
4. Fourth field-trial reading
5. $1 + 2$
6. $1 + 2 + 3$
7. $1 + 2 + 3 + 4$
8. PSAT-verbal
9. Objective subtest, sentence correction
10. Objective subtest, prose groups
11. Objective subtest, construction shift
12. Sum of five original readings of topic A
13. Sum of five original readings of topic B
14. Original total essay minus variable 12
15. Original total essay minus variable 13

For sample A-3 two additional variables were included:

16. Fifth reading
17. $1 + 2 + 3 + 4 + 16$

The intercorrelations of the variables for the four samples are reported in Tables XIV, XV, XVI, and XVII in Appendix B. From the intercorrelations of selected variables, certain relevant relationships can be explored. For example, from sample A-3 the intercorrelation of variables 12 and 17 (.676) provides an estimate of the reading reliability when the score is the sum of five readings. The correlations between variables 13 and 17 (.478) and between variables 12 and 13 (.410) are estimates of the score reliability

Table 13: Design for reading English essays — December 1962

Sample	Table No.	Order of reading I	II	III	IV	V
A-3 (N = 296)						
Topic A, 3-point scale	1	A[a]	E	C	D	B
	2	B	D	E	A	C
	3	C	B	D	E	A
	4	D	C	A	B	E
	5	E	A	B	C	D
B-3 (N = 279)						
Topic B, 3-point scale	6	F	G	H	I	
	7	G	I	F	H	
	8	H	F	I	G	
	9	I	H	G	F	
A-4 (N = 237)						
Topic A, 4-point scale	10	K	L	M	N	
	11	L	N	K	M	
	12	M	K	N	L	
	13	N	M	L	K	
B-4 (N = 254)						
Topic B, 4-point scale	14	P	Q	R	S	
	15	Q	S	P	R	
	16	R	P	S	Q	
	17	S	R	Q	P	

a. Capital letters in the cells of the table refer to packs of approximately 65 papers each, which were moved from table to table for successive readings.

when the score is based on five readings of a single topic. The correlations between variables 12 and 14 (.508), between variables 13 and 15 (.611), and between variables 14 and 17 (.561) are all estimates of the validity of a single essay score based on five readings.

An analysis of variance was carried out on each of the four samples. The results are presented in Tables XVIII, XIX, XX, and XXI in Appendix B. The reliability estimate of the sum of five readings of sample A-3 is .701.

Since there were five field-trial readings for sample A-3 only, direct comparisons among the four samples are possible for four or fewer readings only. In Table 14 are data comparing the reading reliabilities (based on analysis of variance) of the sums of four field-trial readings with corresponding estimates of the sums of four and five of the original readings. Also included are the correlations between the field-trial scores (four readings) and the original readings (five readings). The internal consistency estimates based on four readings are generally a little lower for the field-trial readings; those based on correlations between the two sets of scores are slightly lower than the square roots of the products of the corresponding internal consistency estimates. The differences,

Table 14: Estimates of reading reliabilities of essay ratings: (1) Analysis of variance estimates for sums of four field-trial readings, (2) Analysis of variance estimates for sums of five original readings, (3) Correlations of field-trial scores with original scores

Sample[a]	N	Field-trial readings (1)	Original[b] readings (2)	Field-trial with original (3)
A-3	296	.647	.729 (.683)	.653
B-3	279	.672	.728 (.682)	.668
A-4	237	.714	.754 (.710)	.668
B-4	254	.685	.797 (.759)	.732

a. A-3: Topic A papers, field-trial reading on three-point scale
  B-3: Topic B papers, field-trial reading on three-point scale
  A-4: Topic A papers, field-trial reading on four-point scale
  B-4: Topic B papers, field-trial reading on four-point scale

b. Figures in parentheses are estimates of reading reliabilities of the sums of four readings. All these estimates are based on readings on a three-point scale.

however, are of little practical significance.

At first glance it appears that the reading reliabilities based on a four-point scale (.714 and .685) are better than those based on a three-point scale (.647 and .672). A more detailed study of the data in Table 14 reveals differences of the same or greater magnitude in the column for the original readings, all of which are based on a three-point scale. The differences in reading reliability for samples A-3 and B-3 on the one hand and for samples A-4 and B-4 on the other hand are probably due to differences among the samples rather than to differences in technique of reading. Before drawing final conclusions regarding the efficiency of the four-point scale, however, other data need to be examined.

Table 15 summarizes the evidence with respect to score reliability both for the original sums of five readings on a three-point scale and of the field-trial readings based on the scores of four readers. The reliability coefficients for the field-trial readings range from .418 to .547, those for the original readings from .410 to .447. For three of the four samples, the correlations based on the field-trial readings are higher than those based on the original readings even though scores include one less reading. Furthermore, the score reliabilities based on the four-point reading are higher than for the three-point reading of the same samples of papers. In these comparisons the field-trial readings and the four-point scale are favored.

The primary concern, however, was with validity rather than with reliability. In Table 16 data are

Table 15: *Estimates of score reliabilities of essay ratings: Correlations of sums of four field-trial readings of one topic (A' or B') and of sums of five original readings of same topic (A or B) with sums of five original readings of a second topic (B or A)*

Sample[a]	N	Field-trial		Original	
		$r_{A'B}$	$r_{B'A}$	r_{AB}	r_{BA}
A-3	296	.466		.410	
B-3	279		.418		.419
A-4	237	.547		.447	
B-4	254		.487		.444

a. A-3: Topic A papers, field-trial reading on three-point scale
   B-3: Topic B papers, field-trial reading on three-point scale
   A-4: Topic A papers, field-trial reading on four-point scale
   B-4: Topic B papers, field-trial reading on four-point scale

Table 16: Summary of correlations of objective English scores, field-trial essay scores, and
PSAT-verbal scores with four-essay, 20-reading criterion of writing ability

Sample[a]	N	Objective English subtest			Field-trial essay				PSAT-V
		Sentence correction	Prose groups	Construction shift	One reading	Two readings	Three readings	Four readings	
A-3	296	.665	.528	.584	.384	.477	.531	.542	.562
B-3	279	.666	.512	.603	.337	.470	.521	.574	.631
A-4	237	.673	.557	.630	.446	.551	.603	.634	.689
B-4	254	.675	.557	.589	.454	.490	.596	.640	.628

a. A-3: Topic A papers, field-trial reading on three-point scale
   B-3: Topic B papers, field-trial reading on three-point scale
   A-4: Topic A papers, field-trial reading on four-point scale
   B-4: Topic B papers, field-trial reading on four-point scale

presented showing the correlations of objective English subtests, essays read once, twice, three times, and four times, and PSAT-verbal test on the one hand with an independent criterion of writing ability consisting of scores assigned by 20 readers to four essays on the other hand. The criterion measures are the same as those of Table 12 in the preceding chapter—T_A for the A samples, T_B for the B samples. The picture with respect to the objective English subtests and the PSAT-verbal test is consistent with those presented earlier in this report. Of particular interest at this point are the correlations based on the field-trial reading of the essays. As the number of readings increases, the size of the validity coefficients increases. The coefficients based on one reading range from .337 to .454, those based

on four readings from .542 to .640. The coefficients based on only two readings are larger than the score reliability coefficients based on four readings (Table 15), and those based on three readings are within the range of those based on the objective subtests. It seems clear that scores of practical as well as statistical significance can be obtained under field conditions. Again, the coefficients for the four-point readings average .072 higher than those for the three-point readings. Some of the difference, however, may be attributed to actual differences in the samples; the correlations based on the objective measures are only .031 higher, on the average, for samples A-4 and B-4 than for samples A-3 and B-3.

But were the field-trial scores as valid as the original experimental readings? The data relevant to this question are assembled in Table 17. The coefficients for the original readings are based on the sums of five readings. They range from .508 to .658. Coefficients based on the sums of four field-trial readings range from .542 to .640 and average .011 higher than those for the original readings. It seems reasonable to conclude that there was no loss in validity in moving from experimental to field-trial readings.

The data on reading reliability, score reliability, and test validity for the field-trial readings are assembled in Table 18. Of particular interest is the fact that the validity coefficients for the field-trial samples are consistently higher than the coefficients of score reliability and only a little lower than the coefficients of reading reliability. Validity coefficients range from .542 to .640, depending on the sample and on whether a three-point or a four-point scale

was used. The corresponding coefficients of score reliability range from .466 to .547 and those for reading reliability, from .647 to .714. The figures were surprising when first observed; actually, however, the results should have been anticipated.

In theory, the maximum possible validity for a test is equal to the square root of its reliability; in practice, however, validity coefficients seldom approach in magnitude the reliability coefficients, much less exceed them. In most situations two factors mitigate against high validity coefficients even when both criterion and predictor measures are reliable. One is the fact that tests are usually only indirectly related to the criterion. The other factor is that the criterion is usually highly complex. For example, an attempt is made to try to predict the highly complex criterion of performance in fresh-

Table 17: Correlations of field-trial scores (four readings) and original scores (five readings) on topics A and B with independent four-topic, 20-reading criterion of writing ability

Sample[a]	N	Topic A		Topic B	
		Field-trial score	Original score	Field-trial score	Original score
A-3	296	.542	.508		
B-3	279			.574	.602
A-4	237	.634	.578		
B-4	254			.640	.658

a. A-3: Topic A papers, field-trial reading on three-point scale
   B-3: Topic B papers, field-trial reading on three-point scale
   A-4: Topic A papers, field-trial reading on four-point scale
   B-4: Topic B papers, field-trial reading on four-point scale

man English with a measure of the ability to recognize errors in sentences. It is not surprising that correlations between the two are not high. There is much more to performance in freshman English than the ability to recognize errors in sentences.

In this study, however, the criterion consists of four essays read by 20 readers and the predictor of another essay read by four more readers. The predictor, in other words, is a sample of the same kind of performance as the criterion. Under these conditions, it is inevitable that the correlation between the predictor and the criterion will be higher than the reliability of the predictor. In essence, what we have is the correlation between parallel tests of different length. The longer test (the criterion) is the more reliable and the correlation between the two is approximately equal to the square root of the product of the two reliability coefficients.

This may explain, at least in part, the observation so familiar to everyone in the field of testing, namely that teachers in schools and colleges have seldom been so concerned about the low reliability of essay ratings as have the specialists in testing. Implicitly if not explicitly, the teachers have been accepting the ability to write answers to essay questions as the criterion of school or college learning. And their impressions of the achievement of their students have been based on the sums of their ratings on a large number of written answers over a period of a term or a year. Thus, the discrepancies between criterion measures and test measures (which are a function of the correlation between ratings on a single examination and the sum of ratings on a number of examinations or exercises) are likely to be smaller than the discrepancies between test measures and measures on a single second test (which are a function of the correlation between the two test ratings).

One final question remains to be answered. If the

Table 18: Reading reliabilities, score reliabilities, and test validities of sums of four field-trial readings

Sample[a]	N	Reading reliability	Score reliability	Test validity
A-3	296	.647	.466	.542
B-3	279	.672	.418	.574
A-4	237	.714	.547	.634
B-4	254	.685	.487	.640

a. A-3: Topic A papers, field-trial reading on three-point scale
B-3: Topic B papers, field-trial reading on three-point scale
A-4: Topic A papers, field-trial reading on four-point scale
B-4: Topic B papers, field-trial reading on four-point scale

eld-trial essay scores are substituted for a valid objective subtest in a one-hour composite test, will he new test be more valid than the all-objective one? The data required to answer this question are assembled in Table 19. The multiple correlations based on three objective subtests are .703, .709, .725, and .710. Corresponding coefficients with essay scores based on a single reading are .715, .701, .733, and .736.

In three out of four samples, the substitution of a score based on a single reading increases the multiple correlation. When essay scores based on two readings are used, all four coefficients are higher than those based on the all-objective sections. The average difference is .023 in favor of the test which includes the essay. Corresponding differences for tests which include essays read three times and four times are .036 and .042. When PSAT-verbal scores are added to the composites the multiple correlations are slightly higher and the differences slightly smaller. The beta weights associated with the multiple correlations are presented in Tables XXII and XXIII of Appendix B. As was the case in previous comparisons, the coefficients based on the four-point reading are consistently higher than those based on the three-point reading.

Table 19: Multiple correlations of selected combinations of predictors with four-essay, 20-reading criterion of writing ability

	Predictors[a]									
	(1)	(2)	(3)	(4)	(5)	(6)	(7)	(8)	(9)	(10)
						9	9	9	9	9
	3	3	3	3	3	3	3	3	3	3
	4	4	4	4	4	4	4	4	4	4
Sample[b]	6	1R	2R	3R	4R	6	1R	2R	3R	4R
A-3	.703	.715	.726	.728	.728	.712	.727	.738	.740	.740
B-3	.709	.701	.724	.733	.742	.730	.723	.739	.744	.752
A-4	.725	.733	.752	.767	.770	.754	.759	.771	.782	.784
B-4	.710	.736	.740	.766	.778	.726	.748	.753	.777	.788

a. The following code is used to designate predictors: 3. Sentence correction; 4. Prose groups; 6. Construction shift; 9. PSAT-verbal; 1R. Essay read once; 2R. Essay read twice; 3R. Essay read three times; 4R. Essay read four times.

b. A-3: Topic A papers, three-point scale; B-3: Topic B papers, three-point scale; A-4: Topic A papers, four-point scale; B-4: Topic B papers, four-point scale.

There is no evidence that more time was required for reading on a four-point scale; in fact, the two four-point readings were accomplished in 45 and 54 minutes while the two three-point readings required 56 minutes and 65 minutes. The differences were attributable to delays resulting from failure of the readers' aides to complete the processing of the essay papers between readings and to keep the readers supplied with papers. In spite of the delays, the readers averaged 31 papers in 55 minutes.

5. The measurement of writing ability— a significant breakthrough?

At this point it seems wise to look again at the data in order to assess its full significance. Some interpretations of the data have been presented; however, this series of studies has not been related to the larger context of studies reported previously. The finding that a 20-minute essay does seem to make a unique contribution to the measurement of writing skill appears to be at variance with previous findings. There is danger that the finding may be discounted by some readers and given undue emphasis by others. There is also the danger that other findings of equal significance may be overlooked.

This is not to say that the evidence of the validity of the short essay is not highly significant. It is. In a subsequent study, Myers, Coffman, and McConville (1966) demonstrated that the reading reliability can be maintained even when reading 80,000 essays. As a result the essay is now certified for regular use along with other types of questions in the College Board English Composition Test. But of even greater importance than this practical outcome has been the development of a clearer understanding of the nature of writing skill and of how it can be predicted with a one-hour test. A careful reexamination of the reports cited in Chapter 1 and a study of Vernon's review of research conducted in Great Britain indicate that these findings are not contradictory; in fact, they support conclusions already reached by

Vernon (1957, pp. 120-124). What the study has contributed is a highly reliable criterion measure which permits the relationships to be viewed in sharp focus.

Let us first summarize our procedure. A group of 646 eleventh- and twelfth-grade students wrote on five different topics and took six objective tests of writing ability and two interlinear exercises during a three-week period in October and November of 1961. In December 1961, 25 experienced readers assigned scores of three, two, or one to the essays, each reader assigning one score to each of the subjects. The total of the 25 scores thus assigned became the criterion for evaluating the objective tests and interlinear exercises. The sums of 20 ratings on four of the topics became the criterion for evaluating the fifth topic as a predictor. A year later a group of 145 readers reread two of the topics in order to assess the effects of reading under field conditions involving a large number of readers rather than under experimental conditions involving a limited number of highly experienced readers.

On the basis of the data and in the context of previous research, several broad generalizations seem justified. Each is first stated briefly and then discussed in some detail.

1. *The reliability of essay scores is primarily a function of the number of different essays and the number of different readings included.* If one can include as many as five different topics and have each topic read by five different readers, the reading reliability of the total score may be approximately .92 and the score re-

liability approximately .84 for these samples. In contrast, for one topic read by one reader, the corresponding figures are .40 and .25 respectively. The increases which can be achieved by adding topics or readers are dramatically greater than those which can be achieved by lengthening the time per topic or developing special procedures for reading. Reading reliabilities of approximately .70 were obtained for four readings of a single 20-minute topic. The total reading time required was approximately eight minutes. Noyes, Sale, and Stalnaker (1945) report a median reading reliability of .67 for their one-hour essays read analytically. The reading time was approximately 15 minutes. Swineford (1956) found a reading reliability of .70 for the two-hour General Composition Test read analytically. The reading time was 30 minutes. The reading time is longer for analytical reading and longer essays, but the points of reliability per unit of reading time are greater for short topics read holistically.

2. *When objective questions specifically designed to measure writing skills are evaluated against a reliable criterion of writing skills, they prove to be highly valid.* For the total sample of 646 cases, it was estimated that if five additional essays on parallel topics were read in the same way, the total score would correlate with our criterion approximately .84. With this measure as the criterion, validity coefficients were obtained for five of the six different types of questions ranging from .568 to .709. All composites of three different subtests produced correlations above .70 and the highest was .775. When PSAT-verbal scores

were added, the multiple correlations were even higher, but the increases were small. These findings were in sharp contrast to those of Huddleston (1954) and Diederich (1950) who had obtained multiple correlations of comparable magnitude but with the SAT-verbal score bearing most of the weight. There are two major differences between these findings and those of Huddleston and Diederich: We had a direct measure of writing ability; they used English grades and teacher ratings. We had more refined measures of writing ability, the result of years of developmental work.

One might argue that these findings are attributable to the fact that judgments based on short essays could reflect only the superficial, mechanical aspects of writing skill some critics claim as the functions measured by objective tests of writing ability. A number of different considerations led to rejection of this interpretation. In the first place, the readers testified that they were making judgments on the basis of broader considerations. In the second place, a factor analysis reported by Myers, Coffman, and McConville (1966) supports the hypothesis that the readers were actually making the global judgments for which our directions called. In the third place, the College Board used short essays in 1944, 1945, and 1946. The records from that period provide no evidence of dissatisfaction with the comprehensiveness of the writing skill involved. In fact, the essays were read analytically and seven different qualities were judged. The short essays were dropped because of the difficulty of obtaining reliable scores in the mited amount of time available for reading.

It is not claimed, however, that our criterion measure was in any sense an ultimate one. As in all essays written under test conditions, these place a premium on fluency and ability to write correctly and with some style in a first draft. In actual life situations the writer is seldom under such sharp limitations. He can write and revise. He can consult a dictionary or thesaurus. He can even ask his wife or sweetheart to edit a first draft for him. And he will often have to spend long hours outlining and developing an extensive treatment of a truly complex topic. These samples provide as valid measures of writing *under test conditions* as any that can be obtained in a similar period of time. It would be interesting to collect samples of writing completed over a period of several months under much freer conditions and see how scores based on these samples would be related to the measures we have developed. On the other hand, these are the very kinds of data which provide a basis for teacher's grades and ratings, criteria which have been used in previous studies and which appear to include more emphasis on general verbal ability as measured by the SAT-verbal test. It is doubtful that any additional predictors would be required to obtain multiple correlations of comparable magnitude with such a criterion, but the relative weights assigned to the English and the verbal scores might change significantly.

3. *The most efficient predictor of a reliable direct measure of writing ability is one which includes essay questions or interlinear exercises in combination with objective questions.* The first-order validity coefficients for the interlinear exercises, while not quite so high as those for the most valid objective subtests, are within the same general range; in combination with objective subtests, the interlinear exercises produce generally higher validity coefficients than all-objective combinations. For the essays, the first-order validities do not approach the range of validities for other types of questions until the score is based on three readings. On the other hand, when essay scores are combined with objective subtest scores, they produce validity coefficients even higher than those for the combinations which include an interlinear exercise.

This conclusion regarding efficiency, however, needs some qualification. If considerations of cost are added, the conclusion depends on how much weight is given to cost. The addition to prediction from the 20-minute essay is real but small. The same may be said for the interlinear exercise. Both are expensive to score. It is doubtful that the slight increase in validity alone can justify the increased cost. Rather, the advantage has to be assessed in terms of the model the essay provides for students and teachers. An essay in the English Composition Test says to the student that skill in actual writing is an important outcome of instruction. It says to the teacher that the ability to answer multiple-choice questions, unless accompanied by the ability to compose answers to essay questions, is not sufficient evidence of effective teaching.

This is not to say, however, that the various objective questions included in the English Composition Test are poor models for students and teachers. There are many elements in effective writing, and the attention of the student must be directed to these elements if he is to learn the composite skills. The several exercises were derived from a detailed analysis of the writing process. That the derivations were valid is attested to by the high validity coefficients reported in this monograph. A teacher could do worse than to call students' attention to elements of composition through exercises such as these. It would be unfortunate, however, if the teacher never provided an opportunity for the student to practice putting these elements together.

It should be recalled that one hypothesis of this study was that the multiple-choice questions were discriminating primarily at the lower levels of skill while the interlinear exercise, involving as it does, a total context, would be most suitable at the higher levels. No convincing support for this hypothesis was found. One might argue that these findings would have been different if the students had had an opportunity to edit their own writing. Those who had mastered the several elements of good writing would have eliminated from their papers careless errors which counted against them. This hypothesis should be investigated. On the other hand, there was a suggestion in the data that SAT-verbal scores might be contributing to prediction more heavily among students of high ability. But SAT-verbal scores are based on multiple-choice questions. Before concluding that

objective English questions focus on only superficial aspects of writing ability, one ought to give serious consideration to the data reported here.

Bibliography

Anderson, C. C., "The New STEP Essay Test as a Measure of Composition Ability." *Educational and Psychological Measurement*, Spring 1960, pp. 95–102.

Coffman, W. E., and Papachristou, Judith, "Experimental Objective Tests of Writing Ability for the Law School Admission Test." *Journal of Legal Education*, July 1955, pp. 388–394.

Coward, Ann F., "The Method of Reading the Foreign Service Examination in English Composition." *Research Bulletin RB-50-57*, 1950. Princeton, N. J.: Educational Testing Service, 12 pp. Out of print.

Diederich, Paul B., "Reading and Grading" in *Improving English Composition*. (Arno Jewett and Charles E. Bish, eds.). Washington, D.C.: National Education Association, 1965, Chapter 11.

Diederich, Paul B., "The 1950 College Board English Validity Study." *Research Bulletin RB-50-58*. Princeton, N.J.: Educational Testing Service, 1950, 25 pp. Out of print.

Diederich, Paul B.; French, John W.; Carlton, Sydell T., "Factors in Judgments of Writing Ability." *Research Bulletin RB-61-15*. Princeton, N.J.: Educational Testing Service, 1961, 60 pp. Out of print.

Hopkins, L. Thomas, "The Marking System of the College Entrance Examination Board." *Harvard Monographs in Education*, Series 1, No. 2. Cambridge, Mass.: The Graduate School of Education, Harvard University, October 1921, 15 pp. Out of print.

Huddleston, Edith M., "Measurement of Writing Ability at the College-Level: Objective *vs.* Subjective Testing Techniques." *Journal of Experimental Education*, Vol. XXII, No. 3, March 1954, pp. 165–213.

Miller, Peter, "An Analysis of Error-Types Used in the Interlinear Exercise of the College Entrance Examination Board's English Composition Test." *Eleventh Yearbook*, National Council on Measurements Used in Education (National Council on Measurement in Education), 1953–54, pp. 19–20.

Myers, Albert E.; Coffman, William E.; and McConville, Carolyn B., "Simplex Structure in the Grading of Essay Tests." *Educational and Psychological Measurement*, 1966 (in press).

Noyes, Edward S.; Sale, William M.; and Stalnaker, John M., *Report on the First Six Tests in English Composition*. New York: College Entrance Examination Board, 1945, 72 pp.

Olsen, Marjorie, "Summary of Main Findings on the Validity of the 1955 College Board General Composition Test." *Statistical Report SR-56-9*. Princeton, N.J.: Educational Testing Service, 1956, 43 pp. Out of print.

Olsen, Marjorie, "The Validity of the College Board General Composition Test." *Statistical Report SR-55-4*. Princeton, N.J.: Educational Testing Service, 1955, 27 pp. Out of print.

Pearson, Richard, "The Test Fails as an Entrance Examination." pp. 2–9, in "Should the General Composition Test Be Continued?" *College Board Review*, No. 25, Winter 1955, pp. 2–13.

Sampson, Olive C., "Written Composition at 10 Years as an Aspect of Linguistic Development." *British Journal of Educational Psychology*, Vol. XXXIV, Part 2, June 1964, pp. 143–150.

Swineford, Frances, "College Entrance Examination Board General Composition Test, J." *Statistical Report SR-56-3*. Princeton, N.J.: Educational Testing Service, 1956, 20 pp. Out of print.

Swineford, Frances, "Reliability of an Interlinear Test of Writing Ability." *School and Society*, Vol. 81, No. 2050, January 1955, pp. 25–27.

Swineford, Frances, and Olsen, Marjorie, "Reliability and Validity of an Interlinear Test of Writing Ability." *Research*

Bulletin RB-53-9. Princeton, N.J.: Educational Testing Service, 1953, 6 pp. Out of print.

Thomas, Macklin, "Construction Shift Exercises in Objective Form." *Educational and Psychological Measurement*, Vol. XVI, No. 2, Summer 1956, pp. 181–186.

Vernon, P. E. (ed.), *Secondary School Selection*. London, England: Methuen, 1957.

Weiss, Eleanor S., "The Interrelationships and Validities of Item Types in the College Board English Composition Test." *Statistical Report SR-57-25*. Princeton, N.J.: Educational Testing Service, June 1957, 25 pp. Out of print.

Appendix A

Participating schools, supervisors, and teachers

Sister Mary Roberta, S.S.N.D., principal
  Girls Catholic High School
  366 Charles Street, Malden 48, Massachusetts
    Sister Mary Roberta (grade 12)
    Sister Mary Lucy (grade 11)
Dr. Daniel F. Mahoney, principal
  South Portland High School
  637 Highland Avenue, South Portland, Maine
    Miss Mary J. State, supervising teacher
Mr. James I. Mournighan, principal
  Warwick Veterans Memorial High School
  2401 West Short Road, Warwick, Rhode Island
    Mr. William McDevitt, supervising teacher
Mr. Paul S. Neuman, guidance director
  New Milford High School
  East Street, New Milford, Connecticut
    Mrs. Theo Holt (grade 12)
    Mr. Earl French (grade 11)
Miss Janet Jacobs, dean
  Northfield School for Girls
  East Northfield, Massachusetts
    Eleanor Douglass (grade 12)
    Elizabeth Sanderson (grade 11)
Sister Mary Dionysia, R.S.M., principal
  Mount Saint Mary Academy
  755 Second Street, Fall River, Massachusetts
Miss Mary I. Dwyer, assistant principal
  Pennsbury Senior High School
  Yardley, Pennsylvania
    Miss Marjory Hoffer (grade 11)
    Mrs. Joanne Cardona (grade 12)

Mr. I. L. McDowell, assistant principal
  Parkersburgh High School
  2101 Dudley Avenue, Parkersburg, West Virginia
    Miss Mary Casey Hughes (grade 11)
    Miss Emma Neal Boggess (grade 12)
Mrs. Grier Bartol, headmistress
  The Agnes Irwin School
  Ithan Avenue, Rosemont, Pennsylvania
    Miss Marietta Dean Lent, head of English department
    Mrs. Ashton T. Scott
    Mrs. John C. Keller
Mr. Charles A. Darrah, principal
  Hampton High School
  Allison Park, Pennsylvania
    Kathryn J. Harman, test administrator
Mr. H. G. Williams, principal
  Bellevue High School
  435 Lincoln Avenue
  Bellevue, Pittsburgh 2, Pennsylvania
    Miss Sandra Wolfe (grade 12)
    Miss Mildred E. Wagoner (grade 11)
Mother M. Gonzague, R.S.H.M., principal
  Mother Butler Memorial High School
  1500 Pelham Parkway South, New York 61, New York
    Mother M. Agatha, R.S.H.M.
Mr. Harold D. Babcock, director of guidance
  Wellsville Central High School
  126 West State Street
  Wellsville, New York
    Mrs. Mary K. Baker (grade 11)
    Mr. Charles D. Fuller (grade 12)
Mr. William M. Bush, principal
  Swarthmore High School
  Swarthmore, Pennsylvania
    Miss Mary Armstrong (grade 11)
    Mrs. Hannah Mathews (grade 12)

Miss Helen Pauline Carter, counselor
  William B. Murrah High School
  1400 Murrah Drive, Jackson, Mississippi
    Miss Blanche Musselwhite (grade 12)
    Miss Irene Breland (grade 11)
Dr. Spencer J. McCallie, headmaster
  McCallie School
  Chattanooga 4, Tennessee
Miss Marie S. Yonkman, chairman of English department
  East Grand Rapids High School
  2018 Wealthy Street, S.E., Grand Rapids, Michigan
Dr. Howard D. McEachen, superintendent
  Shawnee Mission High School
  7401 Johnson Drive, Shawnee Mission, Kansas
    Mrs. Wilma White (grade 12)
    Mr. Bob Wootton (grade 12)
    Mrs. Nora B. Cowan (grade 11)
    Mrs. Betty Comstock (grade 11)
Mr. J. H. Rose, principal
  Whitefish Bay High School
  1200 E. Fairmont Avenue, Milwaukee 17, Wisconsin
Mr. Harold T. Lundholm, principal
  The Blake School
  Excelsior Boulevard and Blake Road
  Hopkins, Minnesota
    Mr. William J. Glenn, head, department of English
    Mr. S. Keller Pollock
Mr. Dale O. Rogers, counselor
  Hobbs Senior High School
  P.O. Box 2017, Hobbs, New Mexico
Mr. Eugene R. McSweeney, superintendent
  Hilmar Junior-Senior High School
  Hilmar Unified Schools
  Drawer N, Hilmar, California
    Bernice A. Clark, head, department of English

Miss Ruth Jenkins, headmistress
  The Annie Wright Seminary
  Tacoma 3, Washington
    Mrs. J. E. Monroe (grade 12)
    Mrs. R. E. Pierson (grade 11)
Mr. F. Willard Robinson, principal
  Beverly Hills High School
  241 Moreno Drive, Beverly Hills, California
    Mrs. Pearl Baum (grade 11)
    Mrs. Lucy Helgesson (grade 12)

Appendix B

Appendix tables   *Page*

I.   Correlations among the 25 readings of the five essay topics for the total sample of 646 cases 50

II.   Correlations among English Composition Test subscores and criterion essay scores for total sample of 646 cases 52

III.   Correlations among English Composition Test subscores, PSAT scores, and criterion essay scores for 211 seniors with 1960 PSAT scores 54

IV.   Correlations among English Composition Test subscores, PSAT scores, and criterion essay scores for 262 juniors with 1961 PSAT scores 56

V.   Correlations among English Composition Test subscores, SAT scores, and criterion essay scores for 158 students with SAT scores 58

VI.   Correlations among English Composition Test subscores, PSAT scores, and criterion essay scores for 105 seniors with high scores on "usage" . . . 60

VII.   Correlations among English Composition Test subscores, PSAT scores, and criterion essay scores for 106 seniors with low scores on "usage" 62

VIII.   Correlations among English Composition Test subscores, PSAT scores, and criterion essay scores for 131 juniors with high scores on "usage" . . . 64

IX.   Correlations among English Composition Test subscores, PSAT scores, and criterion essay scores for 131 juniors with low scores on "usage" 66

X.   Regression data for predicting total essay score (T) from the sum of three subtests (X) and PSAT-verbal scores (V) for a sample of 533 cases . . . 68

XI.   Regression data for predicting total essay score (T) from the sum of three subtests (X) and PSAT-verbal scores (V) for a sample of 211 cases . . . 69

XII.   Regression data for predicting total essay score (T) from the sum of three subtests (X) and PSAT-verbal scores (V) for a sample of 262 cases . . . 70

XIII.   Regression data for predicting total essay score (T) from the sum of three subtests (X) and PSAT-verbal scores (V) for a sample of 158 cases . . . 71

XIV.   Correlations among experimental essay scores, objective English subscores, PSAT scores, and criterion essay scores for sample A-3 72

XV.   Correlations among experimental essay scores, objective English subscores, PSAT scores, and criterion essay scores for sample A-4 74

XVI. Correlations among experimental essay scores, objective English subscores, PSAT scores, and criterion essay scores for sample B-3 76

XVII. Correlations among experimental essay scores, objective English subscores, PSAT scores, and criterion essay scores for sample B-4 78

XVIII. Analysis of variance and estimates of reading reliability for sample A-3 . 80

XIX. Analysis of variance and estimate of reliability for sample A-4 81

XX. Analysis of variance and estimate of reliability for sample B-3 82

XXI. Analysis of variance and estimate of reliability for sample B-4 82

XXII. Beta weights for predictors in combinations 1–5 83

XXIII. Beta weights for predictors in combinations 6–10 84

Table I: Correlations among the 25 readings of the five essay topics for the total sample of 646 cases

		Mean	S.D.	Pen pal					Teen-ager				
Topics				a	b	c	d	e	a	b	c	d	e
Pen pal	a	1.87	.69		.412	.349	.415	.367					
	b	1.76	.65	.412		.346	.359	.318					
	c	1.79	.64	.349	.346		.397	.340					
	d	1.82	.64	.415	.359	.397		.357					
	e	1.70	.65	.367	.318	.340	.357						
Teen-ager	a	1.68	.69	.281	.276	.244	.258	.235		.473	.425	.389	.406
	b	1.60	.64	.325	.225	.204	.242	.250	.473		.409	.377	.376
	c	1.62	.67	.249	.226	.235	.261	.193	.425	.409		.419	.415
	d	1.63	.66	.256	.245	.163	.179	.177	.389	.377	.419		.416
	e	1.58	.65	.288	.174	.240	.271	.232	.406	.376	.415	.416	
Imagine	a	2.03	.70	.247	.254	.223	.209	.195	.275	.264	.270	.238	.299
	b	1.87	.65	.288	.256	.282	.246	.209	.315	.310	.274	.185	.243
	c	1.86	.66	.207	.246	.284	.231	.192	.287	.223	.213	.209	.272
	d	1.87	.66	.277	.198	.304	.268	.268	.291	.299	.292	.247	.283
	e	1.78	.66	.294	.224	.209	.276	.159	.250	.271	.255	.186	.285
step 2C	a	1.88	.68	.306	.290	.259	.351	.248	.304	.291	.273	.239	.283
	b	1.81	.65	.252	.216	.249	.258	.253	.296	.289	.271	.222	.276
	c	1.71	.66	.302	.194	.227	.293	.274	.317	.215	.237	.205	.277
	d	1.81	.64	.257	.198	.234	.252	.231	.307	.243	.241	.188	.223
	e	1.73	.65	.259	.214	.228	.222	.250	.313	.280	.301	.251	.270
step 2D	a	1.70	.67	.273	.213	.229	.239	.223	.376	.316	.298	.288	.388
	b	1.60	.64	.262	.243	.246	.242	.202	.365	.314	.298	.282	.324
	c	1.55	.63	.222	.114	.202	.179	.147	.283	.264	.308	.260	.329
	d	1.57	.62	.257	.215	.239	.245	.193	.351	.304	.312	.240	.350
	e	1.57	.63	.258	.228	.252	.205	.204	.340	.268	.281	.254	.299
Total essay		43.40	9.16	.570*	.494*	.514*	.534*	.480*	.622*	.575*	.571*	.511*	.589

* Spuriously high because part is included in the total.

imagine					STEP 2C					STEP 2D				
a	b	c	d	e	a	b	c	d	e	a	b	c	d	e
	.408	.430	.438	.363										
.408		.372	.392	.373										
.430	.372		.380	.349										
.438	.392	.380		.344										
.363	.373	.349	.344											
.257	.278	.285	.274	.241		.375	.395	.350	.358					
.376	.269	.297	.362	.263	.375		.394	.359	.380					
.245	.202	.235	.267	.200	.395	.394		.333	.315					
.226	.200	.251	.212	.231	.350	.359	.333		.352					
.241	.250	.297	.321	.229	.358	.380	.315	.352						
.284	.219	.230	.286	.267	.323	.325	.309	.329	.293		.481	.402	.412	.434
.271	.259	.249	.321	.209	.330	.356	.248	.254	.265	.481		.375	.409	.417
.281	.271	.215	.305	.247	.291	.329	.286	.251	.329	.402	.375		.410	.403
.305	.309	.313	.306	.257	.287	.316	.299	.315	.288	.412	.409	.410		.335
.286	.238	.246	.258	.299	.284	.247	.278	.273	.308	.434	.417	.403	.335	
.568*	.549*	.541*	.589*	.524*	.587*	.596*	.541*	.523*	.560*	.606*	.589*	.549*	.589*	.571*

Table II: Correlations among English Composition Test subscores and criterion essay scores for total sample of 646 cases

	Mean	S. D.	1	2	3	4	5	6
1. Paragraph organization	11.67	6.38		.493	.502	.393	.379	.46
2. Usage	24.24	8.78	.493		.775	.582	.650	.70
3. Sentence correction	27.28	7.85	.502	.775		.586	.621	.73
4. Prose groups	10.53	6.50	.393	.582	.586		.504	.55
5. Error recognition	17.32	6.53	.379	.650	.621	.504		.60
6. Construction shift	17.25	5.62	.462	.702	.730	.554	.601	
7. Interlinear (Valley Forge)	26.76	7.45	.456	.718	.690	.530	.563	.65
8. Interlinear (housefly)	22.73	7.35	.448	.609	.635	.492	.503	.60
T. Total essay score	43.40	9.16	.458	.707	.705	.568	.592	.64
A. Pen pal	8.95	2.29	.335	.535	.503	.399	.403	.43
B. Teen-ager	8.12	2.42	.347	.541	.545	.465	.455	.52
C. Imagine	9.41	2.39	.352	.538	.550	.426	.443	.50
D. step 2C	8.93	2.30	.388	.577	.574	.466	.517	.53
E. step 2D	7.99	2.32	.372	.575	.585	.462	.498	.53

* Spuriously high because part is included in the total.

	8	T	A	B	C	D	E
.456	.448	.458	.335	.347	.352	.388	.372
.718	.609	.707	.535	.541	.538	.577	.575
.690	.635	.705	.503	.545	.550	.574	.585
.530	.492	.568	.399	.465	.426	.466	.462
.563	.503	.592	.403	.455	.443	.517	.498
.655	.608	.645	.436	.521	.503	.530	.531
	.702	.668	.454	.524	.503	.571	.560
.702		.644	.473	.483	.493	.543	.527
.668	.644		.738*	.791*	.777*	.804*	.800*
.454	.473	.738*		.466	.483	.516	.435
.524	.483	.791*	.466		.505	.521	.584
.503	.493	.777*	.483	.505		.523	.520
.571	.543	.804*	.516	.521	.523		.592
.560	.527	.800*	.435	.584	.520	.592	

Table III: Correlations among English Composition Test subscores,
PSAT scores, and criterion essay scores for 211 seniors with 1960 PSAT scores

	Mean	S. D.	1	2	3	4	5	6
1. Paragraph organization	13.42	6.35		.464	.495	.388	.354	.45(
2. Usage	26.72	7.81	.464		.722	.584	.621	.68.
3. Sentence correction	29.43	7.11	.495	.722		.598	.577	.69.
4. Prose groups	11.76	6.48	.388	.584	.598		.505	.54'
5. Error recognition	18.33	6.09	.354	.621	.577	.505		.58.
6. Construction shift	18.35	5.26	.450	.682	.693	.547	.581	
7. Interlinear (Valley Forge)	29.20	6.59	.463	.684	.667	.509	.547	.648
8. Interlinear (housefly)	25.24	7.14	.446	.573	.652	.483	.482	.638
T. Total essay score	46.42	8.79	.478	.640	.653	.580	.573	.61(
A. Pen pal	9.68	2.36	.328	.466	.469	.345	.412	.42.
B. Teen-ager	8.59	2.49	.386	.470	.474	.474	.409	.43
C. Imagine	9.91	2.43	.342	.516	.482	.464	.436	.49(
D. STEP 2C	9.58	2.22	.384	.511	.546	.474	.460	.50]
E. STEP 2D	8.67	2.25	.350	.431	.477	.408	.428	.43(
9. PSAT-verbal score	46.82	10.21	.530	.676	.704	.614	.646	.618
10. PSAT-mathematical score	47.88	9.91	.459	.418	.517	.388	.392	.45(

* Spuriously high because part is included in the total.

7	8	T	A	B	C	D	E	9	10
.463	.446	.478	.328	.386	.342	.384	.350	.530	.459
.684	.573	.640	.466	.470	.516	.511	.431	.676	.418
.667	.652	.653	.469	.474	.482	.546	.477	.704	.517
.509	.483	.580	.345	.474	.464	.474	.408	.614	.388
.547	.482	.573	.412	.409	.436	.460	.428	.646	.392
.648	.638	.610	.423	.434	.490	.501	.436	.618	.456
	.685	.651	.414	.509	.469	.565	.481	.704	.443
.685		.597	.435	.408	.487	.504	.402	.632	.553
.651	.597		.711*	.766*	.755*	.761*	.746*	.697	.411
.414	.435	.711*		.403	.449	.455	.347	.444	.284
.509	.408	.766*	.403		.448	.474	.512	.540	.298
.469	.487	.755*	.449	.448		.452	.457	.497	.262
.565	.504	.761*	.455	.474	.452		.498	.533	.348
.481	.402	.746*	.347	.512	.457	.498		.596	.350
.704	.632	.697	.444	.540	.497	.533	.596		.615
.443	.553	.411	.284	.298	.262	.348	.350	.615	

Table IV: Correlations among English Composition Test subscores, PSAT *scores, and criterion essay scores for 262 juniors with 1961* PSAT *scores*

	Mean	S. D.	1	2	3	4	5	6
1. Paragraph organization	11.30	5.83		.452	.486	.328	.321	.451
2. Usage	24.33	8.06	.452		.714	.480	.569	.628
3. Sentence correction	27.28	7.43	.486	.714		.505	.585	.719
4. Prose groups	10.60	6.40	.328	.480	.505		.415	.466
5. Error recognition	18.21	5.97	.321	.569	.585	.415		.530
6. Construction shift	17.58	5.36	.451	.628	.719	.466	.530	
7. Interlinear (Valley Forge)	27.22	6.74	.361	.639	.632	.454	.464	.565
8. Interlinear (housefly)	22.95	6.49	.338	.490	.541	.397	.378	.516
T. Total essay score	43.78	8.49	.373	.663	.664	.504	.498	.578
A. Pen pal	8.84	2.11	.197	.455	.402	.351	.291	.329
B. Teen-ager	8.23	2.34	.265	.480	.493	.368	.361	.481
C. Imagine	9.61	2.22	.320	.467	.537	.365	.337	.422
D. STEP 2C	9.03	2.13	.303	.518	.508	.405	.443	.460
E. STEP 2D	8.08	2.28	.339	.614	.597	.439	.469	.513
9. PSAT-verbal score	48.46	9.47	.407	.646	.681	.566	.578	.575
10. PSAT-mathematical score	51.23	9.75	.370	.349	.481	.256	.345	.419

* Spuriously high because part is included in the total.

	7	8	T	A	B	C	D	E	9	10
	.361	.338	.373	.197	.265	.320	.303	.339	.407	.370
	.639	.490	.663	.455	.480	.467	.518	.614	.646	.349
	.632	.541	.664	.402	.493	.537	.508	.597	.681	.481
	.454	.397	.504	.351	.368	.365	.405	.439	.566	.256
	.464	.378	.498	.291	.361	.337	.443	.469	.578	.345
	.565	.516	.578	.329	.481	.422	.460	.513	.575	.419
		.595	.577	.338	.427	.433	.477	.529	.534	.367
	.595		.552	.362	.439	.382	.453	.472	.512	.328
	.577	.552		.702*	.789*	.735*	.784*	.815*	.641	.308
	.338	.362	.702*		.426	.411	.471	.413	.432	.099
	.427	.439	.789*	.426		.476	.491	.595	.422	.173
	.433	.382	.735*	.411	.476		.442	.478	.466	.278
	.477	.453	.784*	.471	.491	.442		.615	.549	.340
	.529	.472	.815*	.413	.595	.478	.615		.586	.290
	.534	.512	.641	.432	.422	.466	.549	.586		.483
	.367	.328	.308	.099	.173	.278	.340	.290	.483	

Table V: Correlations among English Composition Test subscores, SAT *scores,*
and criterion essay scores for 158 students with SAT *scores*

	Mean	S. D.	1	2	3	4	5	6
1. Paragraph organization	14.27	6.37		.490	.465	.484	.377	.470
2. Usage	27.12	8.12	.490		.729	.650	.753	.725
3. Sentence correction	29.91	7.00	.465	.729		.613	.646	.697
4. Prose groups	12.59	6.59	.484	.650	.613		.560	.603
5. Error recognition	18.12	6.57	.377	.753	.646	.560		.641
6. Construction shift	19.03	5.53	.470	.725	.697	.603	.641	
7. Interlinear (Valley Forge)	29.44	6.97	.473	.720	.655	.557	.634	.666
8. Interlinear (housefly)	25.94	7.04	.426	.551	.570	.447	.528	.598
T. Total essay score	46.80	8.99	.451	.657	.646	.553	.601	.592
A. Pen pal	9.82	2.28	.320	.521	.491	.341	.453	.451
B. Teen-ager	8.72	2.68	.363	.497	.477	.477	.448	.448
C. Imagine	10.06	2.40	.231	.426	.377	.334	.387	.356
D. STEP 2C	9.52	2.28	.398	.553	.577	.469	.495	.513
E. STEP 2D	8.68	2.39	.373	.461	.499	.438	.467	.447
9. SAT-verbal score	508.04	104.16	.496	.721	.717	.631	.726	.638
10. SAT-mathematical score	533.76	102.78	.430	.497	.508	.381	.427	.480

* Spuriously high because part is included in the total.

7	8	T	A	B	C	D	E	9	10
.473	.426	.451	.320	.363	.231	.398	.373	.496	.430
.720	.551	.657	.521	.497	.426	.553	.461	.721	.497
.655	.570	.646	.491	.477	.377	.577	.499	.717	.508
.557	.447	.553	.341	.477	.334	.469	.438	.631	.381
.634	.528	.601	.453	.448	.387	.495	.467	.726	.427
.666	.598	.592	.451	.448	.356	.513	.447	.638	.480
	.714	.676	.481	.516	.466	.572	.493	.719	.420
.714		.534	.373	.378	.361	.476	.412	.614	.458
.676	.534		.737*	.769*	.709*	.771*	.750*	.633	.322
.481	.373	.737*		.454	.443	.485	.402	.495	.299
.516	.378	.769*	.454		.365	.483	.514	.531	.290
.466	.361	.709*	.443	.365		.452	.397	.370	.084
.572	.476	.771*	.485	.483	.452		.487	.477	.290
.493	.412	.750*	.402	.514	.397	.487		.487	.241
.719	.614	.633	.495	.531	.370	.477	.487		.636
.420	.458	.322	.299	.290	.084	.290	.241	.636	

Table VI: Correlations among English Composition Test subscores, PSAT *scores, and criterion essay scores for 105 seniors with high scores on "usage"*

	Mean	S. D.	1	2	3	4	5	6
1. Paragraph organization	15.33	6.71		.482	.395	.407	.287	.370
2. Usage**	33.29	4.25	.482		.513	.543	.510	.531
3. Sentence correction	33.70	4.98	.395	.513		.518	.415	.523
4. Prose groups	14.83	6.08	.407	.543	.518		.425	.543
5. Error recognition	21.48	5.24	.287	.510	.415	.425		.487
6. Construction shift	21.48	4.05	.370	.531	.523	.543	.487	
7. Interlinear (Valley Forge)	33.11	5.00	.388	.459	.471	.365	.435	.494
8. Interlinear (housefly)	28.66	6.38	.361	.357	.492	.337	.364	.550
T. Total essay score	50.58	8.07	.443	.556	.451	.467	.510	.559
A. Pen pal	10.46	2.24	.174	.296	.244	.175	.339	.381
B. Teen-ager	9.46	2.57	.311	.429	.286	.372	.369	.309
C. Imagine	10.77	2.31	.366	.437	.289	.369	.341	.432
D. STEP 2C	10.51	2.08	.347	.389	.383	.363	.339	.401
E. STEP 2D	9.38	2.19	.373	.412	.409	.370	.418	.471
9. PSAT-verbal score	52.24	9.34	.562	.602	.567	.550	.587	.512
10. PSAT-mathematical score	51.36	10.00	.496	.315	.524	.347	.375	.374

* Spuriously high because part is included in the total.
** Group selected on the basis of scores on this subtest.

	8	T	A	B	C	D	E	9	10
388	.361	.443	.174	.311	.366	.347	.373	.562	.496
459	.357	.556	.296	.429	.437	.389	.412	.602	.315
471	.492	.451	.244	.286	.289	.383	.409	.567	.524
365	.337	.467	.175	.372	.369	.363	.370	.550	.347
.435	.364	.510	.339	.369	.341	.339	.418	.587	.375
494	.550	.559	.381	.309	.432	.401	.471	.512	.374
	.603	.560	.328	.466	.362	.379	.440	.655	.432
.603		.475	.333	.339	.375	.332	.299	.506	.505
.560	.475		.660*	.721*	.709*	.714*	.736*	.670	.365
.328	.333	.660*		.337	.402	.333	.273	.378	.232
.466	.339	.721*	.337		.327	.363	.447	.588	.309
.362	.375	.709*	.402	.327		.383	.400	.415	.173
.379	.332	.714*	.333	.363	.383		.509	.412	.279
.440	.299	.736*	.273	.447	.400	.509		.561	.296
.655	.506	.670	.378	.588	.415	.412	.561		.553
.432	.505	.365	.232	.309	.173	.279	.296	.553	

Table VII: Correlations among English Composition Test subscores, PSAT *scores, and criterion essay scores for 106 seniors with low scores on "usage"*

	Mean	S. D.	1	2	3	4	5	6
1. Paragraph organization	11.53	5.33		.324	.453	.133	.195	.347
2. Usage**	20.22	4.32	.324		.505	.229	.302	.329
3. Sentence correction	25.21	6.34	.453	.505		.400	.379	.529
4. Prose groups	8.73	5.34	.133	.229	.400		.261	.212
5. Error recognition	15.22	5.20	.195	.302	.379	.262		.321
6. Construction shift	15.25	4.43	.347	.329	.529	.212	.321	
7. Interlinear (Valley Forge)	25.33	5.62	.365	.406	.496	.288	.279	.432
8. Interlinear (housefly)	21.86	6.17	.366	.368	.554	.331	.264	.460
T. Total essay score	42.30	7.43	.346	.462	.601	.451	.359	.378
A. Pen pal	8.91	2.23	.359	.443	.456	.291	.262	.227
B. Teen-ager	7.74	2.08	.323	.264	.441	.383	.191	.307
C. Imagine	9.05	2.23	.134	.418	.423	.351	.291	.316
D. STEP 2C	8.65	1.94	.234	.251	.432	.323	.287	.292
E. STEP 2D	7.96	2.08	.165	.232	.362	.241	.230	.190
9. PSAT-verbal score	41.44	7.94	.308	.392	.596	.406	.431	.385
10. PSAT-mathematical score	44.43	8.50	.251	.165	.321	.170	.135	.288

* Spuriously high because part is included in the total.
** Group selected on the basis of scores on this subtest.

	8	T	A	B	C	D	E	9	10
365	.366	.346	.359	.323	.134	.234	.165	.308	.251
406	.368	.462	.443	.264	.418	.251	.232	.392	.165
496	.554	.601	.456	.441	.423	.432	.362	.596	.321
288	.331	.451	.291	.383	.351	.323	.241	.406	.170
279	.264	.359	.262	.191	.291	.287	.230	.431	.135
432	.460	.378	.227	.307	.316	.292	.190	.385	.288
	.539	.493	.255	.346	.328	.489	.337	.499	.195
539		.488	.339	.243	.398	.435	.304	.516	.429
493	.488		.677*	.744*	.717*	.692*	.691*	.509	.213
255	.339	.677*		.318	.350	.409	.271	.291	.145
346	.243	.744*	.318		.430	.420	.464	.250	.047
328	.398	.717*	.350	.430		.329	.378	.361	.138
489	.435	.692*	.409	.420	.329		.329	.394	.183
337	.304	.691*	.271	.464	.378	.329		.501	.239
499	.516	.509	.291	.250	.361	.394	.501		.524
195	.429	.213	.145	.047	.138	.183	.239	.524	

Table VIII: Correlations among English Composition Test subscores, PSAT *scores, and criterion essay scores for 131 juniors with high scores on "usage"*

	Mean	S. D.	1	2	3	4	5	6
1. Paragraph organization	13.45	5.72		.287	.364	.190	.144	.285
2. Usage**	30.96	3.91	.287		.439	.204	.233	.369
3. Sentence correction	31.63	5.15	.364	.439		.254	.343	.536
4. Prose groups	13.18	6.26	.190	.204	.254		.193	.174
5. Error recognition	21.11	4.63	.144	.233	.343	.193		.298
6. Construction shift	20.36	4.10	.285	.369	.536	.174	.298	
7. Interlinear (Valley Forge)	31.12	5.55	.117	.418	.339	.213	.164	.252
8. Interlinear (housefly)	25.85	5.60	.123	.276	.328	.230	.214	.353
T. Total essay score	48.45	7.61	.209	.412	.492	.341	.235	.301
A. Pen pal	9.67	2.04	.008	.248	.196	.219	.012	.046
B. Teen-ager	9.15	2.31	.111	.261	.333	.209	.165	.332
C. Imagine	10.51	2.06	.194	.155	.318	.169	.028	.148
D. STEP 2C	9.91	2.15	.199	.450	.444	.301	.308	.248
E. STEP 2D	9.21	2.19	.224	.339	.442	.307	.303	.273
9. PSAT-verbal score	53.55	7.77	.300	.399	.480	.328	.378	.237
10. PSAT-mathematical score	53.90	8.43	.400	.225	.390	.069	.412	.258

* Spuriously high because part is included in the total.
** Group selected on the basis of scores on this subtest.

7	8	T	A	B	C	D	E	9	10
.117	.123	.209	.008	.111	.194	.199	.224	.300	.400
.418	.276	.412	.248	.261	.155	.450	.339	.399	.225
.339	.328	.492	.196	.333	.318	.444	.442	.480	.390
.213	.230	.341	.219	.209	.169	.301	.307	.328	.069
.164	.214	.235	.012	.165	.028	.308	.303	.378	.412
.252	.353	.301	.046	.332	.148	.248	.273	.237	.258
	.416	.354	.137	.244	.162	.339	.361	.244	.192
.416		.443	.258	.364	.174	.378	.380	.188	.148
.354	.443		.653*	.722*	.623*	.765*	.773*	.451	.120
.137	.258	.653*		.352	.299	.429	.268	.264	.084—
.244	.364	.722*	.352		.274	.380	.498	.197	.025
.162	.174	.623*	.299	.274		.307	.356	.234	.105
.339	.378	.765*	.429	.380	.307		.588	.485	.229
.361	.380	.773*	.268	.498	.356	.588		.417	.146
.244	.188	.451	.264	.197	.234	.485	.417		.452
.192	.148	.120	.084—	.025	.105	.229	.146	.452	

Table IX: Correlations among English Composition Test subscores, PSAT scores, and criterion essay scores for 131 juniors with low scores on "usage"

	Mean	S. D.	1	2	3	4	5	6
1. Paragraph organization	9.15	5.11		.288	.367	.238	.208	.374
2. Usage**	17.69	5.17	.288		.544	.366	.406	.442
3. Sentence correction	22.94	6.79	.367	.544		.473	.474	.640
4. Prose groups	8.01	5.42	.238	.366	.473		.356	.48
5. Error recognition	15.31	5.76	.208	.406	.474	.356		.4
6. Construction shift	14.80	5.02	.374	.442	.640	.482	.422	
7. Interlinear (Valley Forge)	23.31	5.44	.284	.304	.532	.392	.335	.490
8. Interlinear (housefly)	20.06	6.01	.301	.220	.431	.306	.200	.389
T. Total essay score	39.11	6.53	.233	.488	.539	.406	.402	.526
A. Pen pal	8.01	1.83	.126	.259	.266	.239	.227	.264
B. Teen-ager	7.31	1.98	.178	.345	.384	.303	.263	.381
C. Imagine	8.70	2.00	.208	.338	.478	.326	.297	.375
D. STEP 2C	8.15	1.71	.151	.263	.303	.264	.318	.401
E. STEP 2D	6.95	1.75	.151	.515	.456	.290	.313	.433
9. PSAT-verbal score	43.37	8.20	.233	.449	.582	.592	.472	.547
10. PSAT-mathematical score	48.55	10.24	.216	.227	.424	.261	.146	.389

* Spuriously high because part is included in the total.
** Group selected on the basis of scores on this subtest.

	8	T	A	B	C	D	E	9	10
284	.301	.233	.126	.178	.208	.151	.151	.233	.216
304	.220	.488	.259	.345	.338	.263	.515	.449	.227
532	.431	.539	.266	.384	.478	.303	.456	.582	.424
′92	.306	.406	.239	.303	.326	.264	.290	.592	.261
35	.200	.402	.227	.263	.297	.318	.313	.472	.146
)0	.389	.526	.264	.381	.375	.401	.433	.547	.389
	.507	.412	.155	.293	.374	.301	.320	.402	.330
507		.379	.195	.276	.314	.282	.263	.512	.309
412	.379		.605*	.779*	.729*	.687*	.711*	.540	.274
155	.195	.605*		.280	.297	.284	.277	.306	.056
293	.276	.779*	.280		.500	.411	.506	.358	.122
374	.314	.729*	.297	.500		.363	.341	.407	.262
301	.282	.687*	.284	.411	.363		.408	.366	.302
320	.263	.711*	.277	.506	.341	.408		.466	.231
402	.512	.540	.306	.358	.407	.366	.466		.386
330	.309	.274	.056	.122	.262	.302	.231	.386	

Table X: Regression data for predicting total essay score (T) from the sum of three subtests (X) and PSAT-*verbal scores (V) for a sample of 533 cases (r$_{VT}$ = .639)*

Combination of ECT subtests X	Correlation r$_{XT}$	r$_{XV}$	Beta weights $\beta_{XT.V}$	$\beta_{VT.X}$	Multiple correlation	Combination of ECT subtests X	Correlation r$_{XT}$	r$_{XV}$	Beta weights $\beta_{XT.V}$	$\beta_{VT.X}$	Multiple correlation
1, 2, 3*	.713	.714	.524	.265	.737	2, 4, 5	.719	.739	.544	.237	.737
1, 2, 4	.697	.710	.489	.292	.726	2, 4, 6	.726	.723	.552	.240	.744
1, 2, 5	.697	.716	.491	.288	.725	2, 4, 7	.733	.721	.566	.231	.750
1, 2, 6	.696	.691	.488	.302	.730	2, 4, 8	.740	.725	.582	.217	.755
1, 2, 7	.707	.693	.509	.287	.737	2, 5, 6	.718	.720	.535	.254	.739
1, 2, 8	.712	.694	.517	.280	.740	2, 5, 7	.728	.721	.556	.239	.746
1, 3, 4	.689	.716	.474	.300	.720	2, 5, 8	.736	.726	.574	.223	.751
1, 3, 5	.692	.726	.483	.288	.720	2, 6, 7	.731	.701	.556	.250	.752
1, 3, 6	.685	.694	.466	.316	.722	2, 6, 8	.736	.703	.567	.240	.756
1, 3, 7	.705	.703	.505	.284	.733	3, 4, 5	.719	.753	.548	.226	.734
1, 3, 8	.699	.694	.493	.297	.731	3, 4, 6	.716	.727	.533	.252	.737
1, 4, 5	.661	.713	.418	.341	.703	3, 4, 7	.734	.734	.574	.218	.749
1, 4, 6	.658	.683	.416	.355	.708	3, 4, 8	.731	.728	.565	.227	.747
1, 4, 7	.680	.692	.456	.324	.719	3, 5, 6	.714	.730	.529	.253	.734
1, 4, 8	.673	.682	.443	.337	.717	3, 5, 7	.731	.737	.570	.219	.746
1, 5, 6	.663	.694	.423	.345	.708	3, 5, 8	.730	.733	.565	.226	.747
1, 5, 7	.687	.705	.469	.308	.721	3, 6, 7	.728	.711	.554	.246	.748
1, 5, 8	.681	.696	.459	.320	.719	3, 6, 8	.724	.703	.543	.257	.747
1, 6, 7	.680	.672	.457	.332	.723	4, 5, 6	.694	.727	.487	.285	.721
1, 6, 8	.671	.659	.442	.348	.720	4, 5, 7	.713	.733	.528	.252	.733
2, 3, 4	.738	.741	.587	.204	.751	4, 5, 8	.711	.728	.523	.258	.733
2, 3, 5	.732	.739	.572	.216	.746	4, 6, 7	.715	.709	.526	.266	.739
2, 3, 6	.733	.720	.567	.231	.751	4, 6, 8	.710	.701	.515	.279	.737
2, 3, 7	.742	.720	.585	.218	.757	5, 6, 7	.712	.712	.521	.268	.736
2, 3, 8	.747	.723	.597	.208	.761	5, 6, 8	.708	.705	.512	.278	.735

* Subtest numbers are the same as those in previous tables.

Table XI: Regression data for predicting total essay score (T) from the sum of three subtests (X) and PSAT-*verbal scores (V) for a sample of 211 cases (*$r_{VT} = .697$*)*

Combination of ECT subtests X	Correlation r_{XT}	r_{XV}	Beta weights $\beta_{XT.V}$	$\beta_{VT.X}$	Multiple correlation	Combination of ECT subtests X	Correlation r_{XT}	r_{XV}	Beta weights $\beta_{XT.V}$	$\beta_{VT.X}$	Multiple correlation
1, 2, 7	.712	.767	.431	.366	.750	2, 6, 7	.717	.756	.445	.360	.755
1, 2, 8	.707	.756	.421	.379	.749	2, 6, 8	.711	.744	.432	.375	.754
1, 3, 6	.696	.742	.397	.402	.746	3, 4, 6	.714	.753	.437	.368	.754
1, 3, 7	.715	.777	.438	.356	.749	3, 4, 7	.736	.791	.495	.306	.760
1, 3, 8	.698	.752	.399	.396	.745	3, 4, 8	.720	.767	.450	.351	.754
2, 4, 6	.711	.744	.432	.376	.754	3, 5, 6	.711	.764	.430	.368	.750
2, 4, 7	.730	.778	.476	.327	.758	3, 5, 7	.733	.801	.487	.307	.755
2, 4, 8	.726	.768	.465	.340	.758	3, 5, 8	.720	.781	.450	.346	.751
2, 5, 6	.702	.748	.409	.391	.748	3, 6, 7	.724	.770	.462	.341	.757
2, 5, 7	.720	.781	.451	.345	.752	3, 6, 8	.705	.543	.419	.386	.751
2, 5, 8	.720	.774	.450	.348	.753						

Table XII: Regression data for predicting total essay score (T) from the sum of three subtests (X) and PSAT-*verbal scores (V) for a sample of 262 cases (r$_{VT}$ = .641)*

Combination of ECT subtests X	Correlation		Beta weights		Multiple correlation	Combination of ECT subtests X	Correlation		Beta weights		Multiple correlation
	r_{XT}	r_{XV}	$\beta_{XT.V}$	$\beta_{VT.X}$			r_{XT}	r_{XV}	$\beta_{XT.V}$	$\beta_{VT.X}$	
1, 2, 7	.676	.663	.448	.344	.724	2, 6, 7	.708	.682	.506	.296	.740
1, 2, 8	.688	.676	.468	.325	.728	2, 6, 8	.722	.697	.535	.268	.747
1, 3, 6	.651	.671	.402	.371	.707	3, 4, 6	.695	.726	.486	.288	.723
1, 3, 7	.671	.673	.438	.346	.718	3, 4, 7	.705	.719	.505	.278	.731
1, 3, 8	.674	.678	.443	.340	.719	3, 4, 8	.712	.728	.523	.261	.734
2, 4, 6	.709	.724	.515	.268	.733	3, 5, 6	.679	.715	.451	.319	.714
2, 4, 7	.708	.707	.510	.281	.736	3, 5, 7	.694	.713	.482	.298	.725
2, 4, 8	.724	.724	.545	.247	.743	3, 5, 8	.704	.725	.504	.276	.729
2, 5, 6	.692	.712	.477	.302	.723	3, 6, 7	.699	.688	.490	.304	.733
2, 5, 7	.696	.699	.484	.302	.729	3, 6, 8	.705	.696	.501	.292	.735
2, 5, 8	.713	.719	.522	.266	.737						

Table XIII: Regression data for predicting total essay score (T) from the sum of three subtests (X) and PSAT-verbal scores (V) for a sample of 158 cases ($r_{VT} = .632$)

Combination of ECT subtests X	Correlation r_{XT}	r_{XV}	Beta weights $\beta_{XT.V}$	$\beta_{VT.X}$	Multiple correlation	Combination of ECT subtests X	Correlation r_{XT}	r_{XV}	Beta weights $\beta_{XT.V}$	$\beta_{VT.X}$	Multiple correlation
1, 2, 7	.712	.773	.555	.204	.724	2, 6, 7	.719	.777	.575	.186	.729
1, 2, 8	.682	.760	.476	.270	.704	2, 6, 8	.690	.765	.498	.251	.709
1, 3, 6	.676	.742	.461	.290	.704	3, 4, 6	.687	.763	.488	.260	.707
1, 3, 7	.717	.781	.571	.187	.726	3, 4, 7	.729	.802	.621	.134	.733
1, 3, 8	.673	.754	.454	.290	.699	3, 4, 8	.693	.785	.512	.231	.708
2, 4, 6	.686	.759	.486	.263	.707	3, 5, 6	.699	.792	.530	.213	.710
2, 4, 7	.722	.792	.592	.164	.728	3, 5, 7	.735	.824	.666	.084	.736
2, 4, 8	.698	.786	.526	.219	.711	3, 5, 8	.699	.806	.541	.197	.709
2, 5, 6	.689	.777	.500	.244	.706	3, 6, 7	.725	.786	.597	.163	.732
2, 5, 7	.720	.805	.600	.150	.726	3, 6, 8	.683	.761	.480	.267	.705
2, 5, 8	.696	.798	.528	.211	.708						

Table XIV: Correlations among experimental essay scores, objective English subscores, PSAT scores, and criterion essay scores for sample A-3
(Topic A — Pen pal, N=296, reading on a three-point scale)

	Mean	S. D.	1	2	3	4	5	6
1. First reading	1.99	.67		.288	.287	.274	.810	.717
2. Second reading	1.92	.65	.288		.395	.319	.795	.754
3. Third reading	1.84	.64	.287	.395		.328	.424	.752
4. Fourth reading	1.86	.65	.274	.319	.328		.370	.414
5. 1 + 2	3.91	1.05	.810	.795	.424	.370		.916
6. 1 + 2 + 3	5.75	1.45	.717	.754	.752	.414	.916	
7. 1 + 2 + 3 + 4	7.61	1.82	.669	.714	.718	.688	.861	.945
8. PSAT-verbal score	46.32	9.61	.226	.240	.265	.237	.290	.328
9. Sentence correction	27.50	7.53	.323	.315	.436	.346	.398	.483
10. Prose groups	10.53	6.47	.201	.265	.293	.183	.290	.341
11. Construction shift	17.31	5.17	.283	.288	.381	.261	.356	.428
12. Original total score A	8.98	2.20	.461	.391	.524	.444	.532	.619
13. Original total score B	8.04	2.21	.376	.315	.336	.273	.431	.463
14. Total essay − 12	34.31	6.89	.384	.381	.414	.332	.477	.531
15. Total essay − 13	35.25	6.69	.423	.417	.488	.398	.524	.598
16. Fifth reading	1.81	.61	.283	.415	.319	.290	.433	.457
17. 1 + 2 + 3 + 4 + 16	9.43	2.17	.639	.714	.691	.658	.843	.919

7	8	9	10	11	12	13	14	15	16	17
.669	.226	.323	.201	.283	.461	.376	.384	.423	.283	.639
.714	.240	.315	.265	.288	.391	.315	.381	.417	.415	.714
.718	.265	.436	.293	.381	.524	.336	.414	.488	.319	.691
.688	.237	.346	.183	.261	.444	.273	.332	.398	.290	.658
.861	.290	.398	.290	.356	.532	.431	.477	.524	.433	.843
.945	.328	.483	.341	.428	.619	.463	.531	.598	.457	.919
	.347	.509	.337	.434	.652	.466	.542	.618	.467	.968
.347		.616	.543	.592	.323	.430	.562	.543	.206	.348
.509	.616		.541	.733	.429	.505	.665	.659	.245	.495
.337	.543	.541		.486	.306	.434	.528	.501	.161	.327
.434	.592	.733	.486		.356	.447	.584	.570	.225	.427
.652	.323	.429	.306	.356		.410	.508	.717	.462	.676
.466	.430	.505	.434	.447	.410		.783	.611	.310	.478
.542	.562	.665	.528	.584	.508	.783		.938	.381	.561
.618	.543	.659	.501	.570	.717	.611	.938		.442	.642
.467	:206	.245	.161	.225	.462	.310	.381	.442		.673
.968	.348	.495	.327	.427	.676	.478	.561	.642	.673	

Table XV: Correlations among experimental essay scores, objective English subscores, PSAT *scores, and criterion essay scores for sample A-4*
(Topic A — Pen pal, N= 237, reading on a four-point scale)

	Mean	S. D.	1	2	3	4	5
1. First reading	2.46	.80		.324	.467	.334	.813
2. Second reading	2.42	.80	.324		.457	.360	.814
3. Third reading	2.33	.81	.467	.457		.358	.568
4. Fourth reading	2.36	.79	.334	.360	.358		.427
5. 1 + 2	4.88	1.30	.813	.814	.568	.427	
6. 1 + 2 + 3	7.22	1.88	.748	.758	.805	.435	.925
7. 1 + 2 + 3 + 4	9.58	2.35	.725	.730	.780	.698	.894
8. PSAT-verbal score	49.49	10.10	.388	.349	.415	.421	.453
9. Sentence correction	28.73	7.45	.353	.348	.409	.435	.430
10. Prose groups	11.54	6.41	.279	.283	.232	.283	.345
11. Construction shift	18.28	5.79	.313	.355	.363	.327	.410
12. Original total score A	9.41	2.31	.499	.563	.519	.525	.652
13. Original total score B	8.65	2.65	.387	.372	.439	.405	.466
14. Total essay −12	36.48	7.91	.446	.451	.516	.447	.551
15. Total essay −13	37.24	7.49	.487	.518	.550	.491	.618

	7	8	9	10	11	12	13	14	15
.748	.725	.388	.353	.279	.313	.499	.387	.446	.487
.758	.730	.349	.348	.283	.355	.563	.372	.451	.518
.805	.780	.415	.409	.232	.363	.519	.439	.516	.550
.435	.698	.421	.435	.283	.327	.525	.405	.447	.491
.925	.894	.453	.430	.345	.410	.652	.466	.551	.618
	.937	.491	.473	.338	.440	.674	.496	.603	.651
.937		.536	.526	.367	.463	.718	.547	.634	.697
.491	.536		.756	.628	.597	.536	.528	.689	.705
.473	.526	.756		.577	.704	.494	.515	.673	.681
.338	.367	.628	.577		.551	.424	.439	.557	.563
.440	.463	.597	.704	.551		.423	.511	.630	.615
.674	.718	.536	.494	.424	.423		.447	.578	.760
.496	.547	.528	.515	.439	.511	.447		.820	.650
.603	.634	.689	.673	.557	.630	.578	.820		.943
.651	.697	.705	.681	.563	.615	.760	.650	.943	

Table XVI: *Correlations among experimental essay scores, objective English subscores, PSAT scores, and criterion essay scores for sample B-3*
(Topic B — Teen-ager, N = 279, reading on a three-point scale)

	Mean	S. D.	1	2	3	4	5
1. First reading	1.85	.67		.319	.266	.258	.810
2. Second reading	1.83	.68	.319		.398	.411	.814
3. Third reading	1.78	.68	.266	.398		.376	.409
4. Fourth reading	1.78	.72	.258	.411	.376		.412
5. 1 + 2	3.68	1.10	.810	.814	.409	.412	
6. 1 + 2 + 3	5.46	1.51	.710	.772	.747	.469	.912
7. 1 + 2 + 3 + 4	7.24	1.96	.640	.748	.715	.734	.855
8. PSAT-verbal score	48.06	9.56	.390	.334	.384	.420	.445
9. Sentence correction	28.20	7.23	.316	.310	.325	.384	.386
10. Prose groups	11.04	6.45	.287	.194	.252	.353	.296
11. Construction shift	17.98	5.43	.241	.259	.273	.281	.308
12. Original total score A	9.42	2.23	.257	.325	.286	.321	.359
13. Original total score B	8.44	2.31	.437	.490	.458	.515	.571
14. Total essay −12	35.63	7.17	.388	.469	.444	.521	.528
15. Total essay −13	36.61	6.95	.337	.425	.398	.470	.470

6	7	8	9	10	11	12	13	14	15
.710	.640	.390	.316	.287	.241	.257	.437	.388	.337
.772	.748	.334	.310	.194	.259	.325	.490	.469	.425
.747	.715	.384	.325	.252	.273	.286	.458	.444	.398
.469	.734	.420	.384	.353	.281	.321	.515	.521	.470
.912	.855	.445	.386	.296	.308	.359	.571	.528	.470
	.944	.497	.427	.329	.347	.390	.622	.584	.521
.944		.539	.472	.384	.372	.418	.670	.641	.575
.497	.539		.661	.594	.582	.441	.496	.634	.631
.427	.472	.661		.527	.712	.425	.505	.677	.666
.329	.384	.594	.527		.485	.350	.421	.524	.512
.347	.372	.582	.712	.485		.387	.469	.615	.603
.390	.418	.441	.425	.350	.387		.419	.530	.729
.622	.670	.496	.505	.421	.469	.419		.785	.612
.584	.641	.634	.677	.524	.615	.530	.785		.940
.521	.575	.631	.666	.512	.603	.729	.612	.940	

Table XVII: Correlations among experimental essay scores, objective English subscores, PSAT scores, and criterion essay scores for sample B-4
(Topic B — Teen-ager, N = 254, reading on a four-point scale)

	Mean	S. D.	1	2	3	4	5
1. First reading	2.25	.89		.330	.330	.431	.821
2. Second reading	2.12	.87	.330		.263	.362	.810
3. Third reading	2.11	.86	.330	.263		.398	.365
4. Fourth reading	2.12	.85	.431	.362	.398		.487
5. 1 + 2	4.37	1.43	.821	.810	.365	.487	
6. 1 + 2 + 3	6.47	1.92	.760	.722	.720	.541	.909
7. 1 + 2 + 3 + 4	8.59	2.48	.735	.681	.693	.760	.869
8. PSAT-verbal score	47.37	10.36	.379	.232	.333	.357	.376
9. Sentence correction	27.88	7.83	.331	.266	.360	.393	.367
10. Prose groups	10.92	6.48	.300	.240	.307	.334	.332
11. Construction shift	17.48	5.52	.253	.271	.307	.326	.321
12. Original total score A	8.91	2.26	.360	.183	.408	.449	.334
13. Original total score B	8.17	2.56	.548	.463	.547	.542	.621
14. Total essay − 12	34.88	7.70	.506	.424	.549	.545	.571
15. Total essay − 13	35.61	7.28	.454	.343	.516	.526	.490

	7	8	9	10	11	12	13	14	15
760	.735	.379	.331	.300	.253	.360	.548	.506	.454
722	.681	.232	.266	.240	.271	.183	.463	.424	.343
720	.693	.333	.360	.307	.307	.408	.547	.549	.516
541	.760	.357	.393	.334	.326	.449	.542	.545	.526
909	.869	.376	.367	.332	.321	.334	.621	.571	.490
	.958	.429	.435	.385	.377	.432	.708	.672	.596
958		.454	.471	.411	.403	.487	.732	.705	.640
429	.454		.700	.577	.614	.419	.479	.629	.628
.435	.471	.700		.593	.728	.502	.519	.663	.675
.385	.411	.577	.593		.557	.382	.459	.566	.557
.377	.403	.614	.728	.557		.395	.499	.606	.589
.432	.487	.419	.502	.382	.395		.444	.561	.749
.708	.732	.479	.519	.459	.499	.444		.824	.658
.672	.705	.629	.663	.566	.606	.561	.824		.943
.596	.640	.628	.675	.557	.589	.749	.658	.943	

Table XVIII: Analysis of variance and estimates of reading reliability for sample A-3
(N=296, topic A read on a three-point scale)

	ss	df	ms	F
Five readings:				
Between cases	279.6730	295	0.9480	3.34**
Between readings	5.7771	4	1.4443	5.09**
C x R	335.0229	1180	.2839	
Total	620.4730	1479		
First four readings:				
Between cases	244.5236	295	0.8289	2.83**
Between readings	3.7331	3	1.2444	4.26**
C x R	258.7669	885	.2924	
Total	507.0236	1183		

** Significant at the 1 percent level.

Reliability of sum of five readings $\dfrac{.9480 - .2839}{.9480} = .701$

Reliability of sum of first four readings $\dfrac{.8289 - .2924}{.8289} = .647$

Table XIX: Analysis of variance and estimate of reliability for sample A-4
(N= 237, topic A read on a four-point scale)

	ss	df	ms	F
Between cases	325.9515	236	1.3812	3.49**
Between readings	2.4009	3	0.8003	2.02
C x R	280.0991	708	0.3956	
Total	608.4515	947		

** Significant at the 1 percent level.

Reliability of sum of four readings $\dfrac{1.3812 - 0.3956}{1.3812} = .714$

Table XX: Analysis of variance and estimate of reliability for sample B-3
(N = 279, topic B read on a three-point scale)

	ss	df	ms	F
Between cases	267.2276	278	0.9613	3.04**
Between readings	1.1254	3	0.3751	1.19
C x R	263.3746	834	0.3158	
Total	531.7276	1115		

** Significant at the 1 percent level.

Reliability of sum of four readings $\dfrac{.9613 - .3158}{.9613} = .672$

Table XXI: Analysis of variance and estimate of reliability for sample B-4
(N = 254, topic B read on a four-point scale)

	ss	df	ms	F
Between cases	391.8543	253	1.5488	3.17**
Between readings	3.4370	3	1.1457	2.35
C x R	370.5630	759	0.4882	
Total	765.8543	1015		

** Significant at the 1 percent level.

Reliability of sum of four readings $\dfrac{1.5488 - .4882}{1.5488} = .685$

Table XXII: Beta weights for predictors in combinations 1 – 5

| | | Beta weight | | | | | | | |
| | | Objective English | | | Essay | | | | |
Combination	Sample	Sentence correction (a)	Prose groups (b)	Construction shift (c)	One reading (d)	Two readings (e)	Three readings (f)	Four readings (g)	Multiple correlation
1 (a, b, c)	A-3	.426	.217	.166					.703
	B-3	.411	.190	.218					.709
	A-4	.382	.197	.253					.725
	B-4	.440	.212	.150					.710
2 (a, b, d)	A-3	.481	.231		.182				.715
	B-3	.523	.204		.113				.701
	A-4	.465	.227		.218				.733
	B-4	.476	.204		.235				.736
3 (a, b, e)	A-3	.456	.213			.234			.726
	B-3	.476	.194			.229			.724
	A-4	.426	.209			.296			.752
	B-4	.466	.196			.254			.740
4 (a, b, f)	A-3	.430	.210				.252		.728
	B-3	.456	.185				.265		.733
	A-4	.383	.218				.348		.767
	B-4	.422	.173				.346		.766
5 (a, b, g)	A-3	.417	.215					.257	.728
	B-3	.435	.166					.307	.742
	A-4	.354	.217					.368	.770
	B-4	.397	.162					.387	.778

Table XXIII: Beta weights for predictors in combinations 6–10

| | | Beta weight | | | | | | | | |
| | | Objective English | | | Essay | | | | | |
Combination	Sample	Sentence correction (a)	Prose groups (b)	Construction shift (c)	One reading (d)	Two readings (e)	Three readings (f)	Four readings (g)	PSAT-V (h)	Multiple correlation
6	A-3	.380	.175	.127					.158	.712
(a, b, c, h)	B-3	.313	.110	.178					.255	.730
	A-4	.192	.104	.237					.337	.754
	B-4	.336	.162	.113					.230	.726
7	A-3	.401	.178		.179				.178	.727
(a, b, d, h)	B-3	.407	.123		.072				.261	.723
	A-4	.279	.136		.200				.325	.759
	B-4	.376	.159		.208				.194	.748
8	A-3	.378	.162			.229			.175	.738
(a, b, e, h)	B-3	.383	.125			.187			.220	.739
	A-4	.272	.133			.261			.282	.771
	B-4	.359	.149			.232			.203	.753
9	A-3	.348	.156				.250		.181	.740
(a, b, f, h)	B-3	.375	.124				.221		.199	.744
	A-4	.248	.148				.310		.256	.782
	B-4	.327	.132				.324		.184	.777
10	A-3	.338	.163					.254	.178	.740
(a, b, g, h)	B-3	.363	.112					.263	.183	.752
	A-4	.229	.150					.327	.246	.784
	B-4	.307	.122					.366	.177	.788